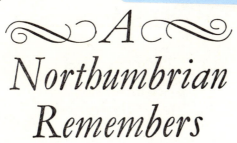

A Northumbrian Remembers

NANCY RIDLEY

Foreword by
DAME IRENE WARD

ROBERT HALE · LONDON

© *Nancy Ridley 1970*
First published in Great Britain 1970

ISBN 0 7091 1830 9

Robert Hale & Company
63 Old Brompton Road
London S.W.7

PRINTED IN GREAT BRITAIN
BY EBENEZER BAYLIS AND SON LTD
THE TRINITY PRESS, WORCESTER, AND LONDON

A NORTHUMBRIAN REMEMBERS

Portrait of Northumberland

Northumbrian Heritage

Contents

Illustrations

PICTURE CREDITS

The writer: 1, 2, 3, 8, 9, 20, 21, 22, 23, 24; Mr Arthur Holmes: 4, 5, 12, 13; The National Portrait Gallery: 6; Scottish Brewers: 7; Sir Charles Orde: 10; Captain Francis Widdrington: 11; Mrs Neville Hadcock: 14; Mr D. H. A. Sleightholme: 18, 19; Mr Alfred B. Stait: 15; Newcastle *Chronicle and Journal*: 16, 17.

Foreword

The authoress has given us a fascinating addition to the saga of Northumberland. Her several contributions on our county's history, inclusive of archaeology, scenery and overall attractions have created a special Northumbrian reading public to which I am delighted to belong, and this—her latest book—has now peopled the hills, the moors and valleys with many of the remarkable men and women who also are part of our heritage.

Northumberland has been wonderfully portrayed by Nancy Ridley, a descendant herself of a very interesting family and in this book she emphasizes the variety of personalities who have indeed created our personal story. Northumberland is a unique county and this characteristic is reflected in the lives of those Nancy Ridley so admirably describes. Each book she has written presents a new facet of our life to her ever increasing number of readers.

My pleasure in writing this foreword is enhanced by knowing the book will be widely welcomed and appreciated by those who value Northumberland's romantic history and undiminished contribution in many spheres to the life of our country.

Irene Ward,

Author's Note

This, my third book on Northumberland, like its predecessors is neither a comprehensive history nor a guide-book, it is a fulfilment of a life-long ambition to pay tribute to the county and its people whom I love so dearly.

"Portrait of Northumberland" and "Northumbrian Heritage" have made me many new friends and opened many doors.

The more I see and learn about Northumberland, the more aware I am that there is still so much to explore and so much I do not know.

I wish to express my heartfelt thanks to my friends old and new who have helped me in so many different ways. Their advice and criticism has been invaluable and they have helped in practical ways by lending me precious books and documents and inviting me into their homes. Last but by no means least, I thank those long-suffering friends who have corrected and proof-read my manuscripts.

Nancy Ridley
Wylam,
Northumberland.

Preface

Having been asked so many times how I can possibly find material to write yet another book about Northumberland, and how my interest in history began, I feel that some explanation is necessary.

The answer to the first question is that even if a whole lifetime was devoted to writing about this most historic county in the British Isles, the result would still be incomplete. Since the coming of the Romans until the present day, Northumberland has made history.

Situated as it is between two countries which for hundreds of years waged bitter warfare, it has on many occasions been 'occupied' territory, thus it is the county of fortresses, dominated by the great castle of Alnwick.

The variety of Northumberland's scenery is such that it could appropriately be called the county of contrasts, yet to many it still remains 'the unknown county'. This unfortunately does not apply to 'foreigners' only, there are many people who have been born and bred in the county who are unaware of their heritage. It has horrified the writer on many occasions to meet and talk with Northumbrians, who though they may have travelled widely abroad know little or nothing of the beauty on their own door-step.

There are on the other hand, the dedicated Northumbrians—and I readily admit to being one—who have a passionate love for this outpost of England, and who take an adverse criticism of the land between Tyne and Tweed as though it were an insult directed at themselves!

Many long years ago when the writer of this book was a small girl she was sent to her room for announcing to a roomful of older people that "Northumberland is the most wonderful place in the world". Her father's crushing words are still remembered:

"You have never been anywhere else!" Now as a middle-aged woman she still holds the same opinion although she has travelled hundreds of miles in the British Isles and seen some of the continent of Europe. The sight of the sun rising over the Alps and the first sight of the Cuillins are outstanding memories, but the magic of Northumberland remains.

When was the interest in history awakened? Largely by the father who so rightly crushed his precocious daughter! Those were still the days when children were seen and not heard, and the quotation "God bless the squire and his relations, and keep us in our proper stations" was still apt.

Coming of a family that has always (with the exception of Matthew Ridley of Peel Well) shunned publicity, the writer has until now said that she would never write about herself, but since developing into that curious creature known as a writer ("We expect you to be odd, you write books," was a remark made to her when *Portrait of Northumberland* was first published) so many questions have been asked and so many misconceptions circulated that it now seems that the time has come to attempt to answer some of the questions. If any reader imagines that startling revelations are going to be made, they are warned now they will be sadly disappointed. There is nothing more distasteful and nauseating than the people who for cheap sensationalism bare their souls in public. They are as abhorrent to this writer as those who decry their parents and blame others for their mistakes and misfortunes.

It is unfashionable nowadays to be proud of one's family or of one's country, and to admit to these feelings is to be labelled a 'square' and a reactionary. Pride of family is not necessarily pride of birth. They are two very different things. It is to the generation who have gone before us that we owe an obligation.

Without the help of my father Robert Ridley I would never have had the abiding love and knowledge of history which has given me so much happiness and satisfaction. One treasured memory is of him buying a horse on the Scottish Border and of the day Pincher first came to my home at Lipwood Well. (Incidentally Lipwood Well is mentioned in the Pipe Roll of Northumberland as being a farm in 1583. It then consisted of eighty acres and was farmed by a John Mason. Today the acreage is about 200.) I was so small that I was lifted onto the horse's back, perched on a green cushion, and led round the yard. When I was told that Pincher had come from a farm on the Border Esk where Prince Charlie crossed into Cumberland in the '45, my interest in Jacobite history began; an interest which has led me "over the sea to Skye" and back to Culloden. My love of history was helped and fostered by my governess, I belong to that period when it was still usual for children to receive the early part of their education at home, and I owe a debt of gratitude to 'Pattie'. How she bore with me for seven years it is hard to understand. I had a rather disobedient pony Captain, and poor 'Pattie' would lead me out on tours of exploration. Sometimes we went as far as the Roman Wall by horse and trap, and the horse was stabled at 'The Twice Brewed' while we scrambled about Housesteads. My mother used to accompany us on these long expeditions. She was a far better horsewoman than I have ever been. I have a photograph of her sitting in a very smart 'turn-out', wearing what was called an Inverness cape and looking very proud and important. This particular horse developed a habit of rearing when in harness, or so I was always told, and he was therefore sold to the Vicar of Beltingham, who christened me! I never discovered if Neddy upset the vicarage family. Beltingham has always had a special place in my affections, for it was there my god-father Uncle George Pearson lived. He and Aunt Lydia had no children of their own, and Uncle George indulged me in many ways. He was responsible to a certain extent for my love of horses and racing—much, I may say, to Aunt Lydia's disapproval. She regarded such sport as a work of the devil, but we managed to slip away to many a point-to-point, though I was always warned that "Your Aunt mustn't know we've been betting". I regarded Uncle George as a Very Important Person because he was a J.P. I had no idea what it meant, and strangely no one ever explained, and for some reason I thought it was to do with the jays I could hear calling in the Lees Wood! Even today when I go racing if a horse has a historical name I back it against all the form; as I know to my sorrow when Grey of Fallodon ran second in The Northumberland Plate.

That name was magic to me as a child. Although my family was Tory an exception was made in the case of Lord Grey. (Usually Liberals were beyond the pale because they were often 'chapel' and teetotal, and that, at least in Grandfather Ridley's eyes, damned them for ever.) In the summer of 1969 when stood I in the woods at Fallodon beside the place where Grey's ashes are buried, I thought how many years it had taken me to come to the end of his story.

Little did I dream in those long ago days when I was for ever pestering people to tell me about the history of Northumberland that I would ever have the thrill of seeing my name in print. Not long ago I found a most extraordinary literary effort, entitled "The Lipwood News", editor N. Ridley. It consists largely of dramatic accounts of the births, marriages and deaths of horses, dogs and cats, and is reminiscent of a well-known local newspaper. All the animals were of course named after historical characters, whether appropriate or not. A favourite cat was Tom Forster of the '15: Unfortunately "The Lipwood News" reports that Dorothy Forster his sister was drowned in a bucket of milk, while Lloyd-George met his death in a cat fight! (I may say the latter was not owned by me.)

For many years my father was a semi-invalid, and he would talk to me for hours about my favourite subject. What infinite patience he must have had to explain and teach me so much. I remember my first visit to Alnwick, and the thrill of at last seeing the castle where Hotspur was born. I felt very grown-up and worldly as, accompanied by my father, we went to 'The White Swan', where I had the first drink of my life, a cider. Everywhere the trail led to history. Over the Border by way of the Carter Bar we travelled —to Kelso, to The Highland Show—and ended up at Gretna Green.

My father's sister, Aunt Annie, was very fond of the Morpeth district—she was at boarding school there—and it was from this aunt I first heard about someone whose name was Emily Davison. It was a very confused story and I had no idea what a suffragette was, apart from the fact that they were'nt 'nice' women and that Emily had hurt a horse. Could that be the reason why I am somewhat anti-Emily even now? Now that I have tried to tell the story of that tragic woman's career I still have the feeling that she wasn't a 'nice' woman.

My interest in Josephine Grey—or Butler, as she became— started in quite a different way. In Haydon Bridge Town Hall there was held a 'Pageant of Nobel Women', and a very pretty dark-haired young woman whom I admired from afar played the part of Josephine Butler. I am quite sure that had Constance, as she was called, known where Josephine's social work lay she would have fled in horror. The word prostitute would not even be in her vocabulary. For many years my mental picture of the great social reformer was that of a pretty young woman wearing a lilac-coloured dress in Haydon Bridge Town Hall.

My first visit to a real castle was to a tea party at Langley, and it is thanks to the niece of Mrs. C. J. Bates, Mrs. Neville Hadcock, that I have been able to use first-hand information about the restoration of Langley. It was at Langley that I saw the now Dame Irene Ward for the first time. There was a Conservative Fête, I was selling button-holes, and the pretty Miss Ward, who made a speech, actually bought a button-hole from me. I remember she was wearing brown, and when I heard that she was a prospective parliamentary candidate I immediately decided that politics would be my career. For weeks afterwards I harangued anyone who would listen to me, not that I knew one word I was talking about. With hindsight I am sure the political scene would not have been enhanced by me. This happy period of my life was nearing its end, and with the death of my father and the wrench of leaving Lipwood Well for the unknown life in a city, history and writing had to recede into the background.

All through the war whenever I had leave it was back to the country I went, to Blanchland, to the beloved Beltingham and the Roman Wall. Now, after more than a quarter of a century, I have achieved my ambition, I have written a tribute to my county.

I have no compunction in devoting the first chapter in this book to 'my' Ridley's. Without the background they gave me, and without the love and encouragement of both my parents, I could never have accomplished so much.

I have now come back to the Tyne Valley I love so dearly, where, sustained by many good and staunch friends who have borne with great fortitude the birth-pangs of my literary efforts, I feel that the long hard road has been worth it all.

This book is more personal that its predecessors. I have written it not only for my county but to please myself, so that I can relive the happy years of my youth. It is a far cry from being editor of "The Lipwood News" to being 'a writer'. I am proud and grateful, and so my family would be if they could share in my efforts to pay a tribute to Northumberland.

For Victoria, Alice and William

I

The Writer's Family

Happy the man, whose wish and care
A few paternal acres bound,
Content to breathe his native air
In his own ground.

Alexander Pope

Much has been written about the great and the famous and about
the very poor, but very little has been written about ordinary
families. Perhaps this is because so many people regard themselves
as ordinary and would rather read about entirely different ways of
life. Yet it is 'ordinary' families who have been the backbone of
this country. Elizabeth I had the insight to realize how important
the middle classes were; and, although today it is more or less
heresy to mention the word 'class', that much-abused term middle-
class is applicable to the majority of English people.

My own family is an example of this type, and, as I am the
last of my particular branch of the Ridleys, I want to put on
record how such a family has lived for many generations in their
native county of Northumberland. Very few families, apart from
the great landowners, have lived out their lives for hundreds of
years in the same district. Since the late seventeenth century I
can find no record of my paternal ancestors ever leaving that
part of South Tynedale in which they were born. In the Parish
Register in Haltwhistle Church appear the births, marriages and
deaths of men and women who never moved further afield than
farms and hamlets within the parishes of Haltwhistle and Beltingham. (There are no marriages recorded at Beltingham before
1881.) This surely is unique. The roots must have been very deep
—or were they an unenterprising family, content to stay among
familiar surroundings and knowing no other way of life? I should
imagine from what I have been told that they were perfectly

happy, and perhaps after the many centuries of raiding and 'lifting' they were glad to settle down and lead a peaceful life.

The first mention of the Ridleys in Northumberland is in the thirteenth century. The name originates from the hamlet of Ridley, which is on the road from Ridley Bridge to Beltingham. The Chief of the Clan lived at the tower of Willimoteswick, the gatehouse of which is still standing.

I have used the word clan purposely, although it is usually applied only to Highland families. Certainly in North Tynedale these family relationships existed in the form of 'The Four Graynes (or clans)': Robsons, Dodds, Charltons and Milburns; and in South Tynedale the Ridleys were at one time the most powerful and numerous family.

The lesser members took orders from the Chief and acted as Searchers and Setters in those troublesome times. The most famous of the sixteenth-century Ridleys was Nicholas the martyr, of whom everyone bearing the name is justly proud, however tenuous the link may be. In 1955 a memorial service was held in the church of St. Mungo at Simonburn in North Tynedale to commemorate the anniversary of the Marian martyr's death. More than a hundred people either bearing the name or connected with the family attended the simple and impressive service when the first and second lessons were read by Mr. John Ridley and the late Viscount Ridley respectively.

Assisting at the service was the Vicar of Delaval, whose name was also Ridley. It was most impressive to listen to the congregation singing the well-known hymn:

> Through the night of doubt and sorrow
> Onward goes the pilgrim band,
> Singing songs of expectation,
> Marching to the Promised Land.
> Clear before us through the darkness
> Gleams and burns the guiding light;
> Brother clasps the hand of brother,
> Stepping fearless through the night.

I have often wondered why Simonburn Church was chosen instead of Beltingham, where Nicholas Ridley is reputed to have been christened. Possibly it was because Doctor Robert Ridley, the uncle of the future bishop, held the living of Simonburn; and in St. Mungo's is a memorial to the bishop's nephew Cuthbert, who was Rector of Simonburn from 1604 until 1636.

In 1967 a service on a much smaller scale was also held in the same church. The memorial outside Balliol College, Oxford is close to the place where Ridley and Latimer met their terrible deaths, and on 16th October 1969 the writer paid her homage there. A strange mixture were these Ridleys of long ago, always until the sixteenth century living on their not inconsiderable lands, 'keeping the peace' (in many cases a misnomer), not above a bit of 'lifting' on the side, and producing some notorious characters as well as distinguished churchmen.

In the sixteenth century some Ridleys were already leaving South Tynedale; and about the time of the Civil Wars the family as a clan disintegrated, some venturing as far afield as Newcastle and ultimately founding the illustrious family at Blagdon of which the fourth Viscount is head today. Others broke into what could be described as splinter groups, some remaining in their native South Tynedale, while others made their new homes in the valley of the North Tyne. Most of these Ridleys carried on the family tradition of farming.

The late Mr. Percy Hedley of Simonburn, whose knowledge of the ramifications of the county families was phenomenal has traced the family in all its varying branches; this must have been a most difficult task, as the same Christian names occur generation after generation. Nicholas—as one would expect, after the most famous of them—is the most common, while William, John, Thomas, Matthew, and Robert are close seconds. My great-grandfather and my grandfather were both christened Matthew, while my father's name was Robert.

It has been a most fascinating experience to attempt to trace my own particular branch, in which I received great assistance from the Vicar of Haltwhistle, the Rev. J. H. Watson, now an honorary canon of Newcastle Cathedral. I must admit that I started with a great advantage as I had always been interested in the people who had given me my background, and as a child I was told so many stories (some of them doubtless apocryphal) of my Ridley ancestors. As the only surviving child of middle-aged parents (I really should have died about twenty years ago had my parents been younger when I was born), I can span the years better than many people of my generation. My father was the youngest of a large family, his eldest sister being twenty-five years older than he, therefore my aunts and uncles could have been my 'greats'. This is proved by the photograph of my Aunt Jane as a Victorian schoolgirl.

After the break up of the clan, the majority of the Ridleys remained on the land as farmers, and until the end of the eighteenth century many of them appear in local records as freeholders. It is, to me at least, a delight to discover that practically every farm mentioned in these records is still a farm today, which shows in many ways how little Northumberland has changed. Willimoteswick, Hardriding, Thorngrafton and Birkshaw, to mention only a few, are still farms, though methods of farming have changed out of all recognition. Yet the glorious countryside in that part of South Tynedale remains unspoilt, and is as yet safe from the 'developers'.

After much detective work I have tracked down my first 'direct' ancestor—which sounds a contradiction in terms, but seems to be the only way in which I can describe my search. On the high ground north of Bardon Mill where the land rises steeply towards the Barcombe range is the hamlet of Thorngrafton, and there somewhere in the late seventeenth century was born Nicholas Ridley, the first whom I can claim without contradiction as the founder of my 'ordinary' branch of the family. On 4th March in the year 1700, when Dutch William's reign was drawing to its close, Nicholas Ridley married Elizabeth Hodgen of 'Ye Millhouse' in the church of The Holy Cross at Haltwhistle, where in the twentieth century I was confirmed. 'Ye Millhouse' at Bardon Mill is still a farm today. Nicholas must have left Thorngrafton to live there after his marriage, as in a list of freeholders for 1734 we find: "Nich. Ridley, Millhouse. On 3rd Dec. 1701 Robert Mallabar of Thorngrafton conveyed Millhouse, par. Haltwhistle to N. Ridley of Millhouse."

At that time Bardon Mill and Henshaw were still part of Haltwhistle parish. The Church of All Hallows at Henshaw was yet to be built and Beltingham Church was in a ruinous condition. Now there is a separate parish of Beltingham-with-Henshaw.

It would appear that Nicholas Ridley's life was in no way disturbed by the Rebellion of the '15, as he was still living peacefully at 'Ye Millhouse' in 1734, though he must have been aware of that pathetic attempt to restore the Stuarts, which has in

Northumberland become the Derwentwater Story. Although the marriage of Nicholas and Elizabeth took place in 1700, it is not until April 1731 that the baptism of their son John appears in the parish register. This can possibly be explained by the fact that in those long ago days baptisms were often postponed for years, sometimes until marriage. Whatever his age, John's parents made sure that their son was made a member of the Church of England; and in January of 1750 John Ridley was married in the same church to Anne Armstrong of the parish of Haltwhistle. This John, my great-great-great-grandfather was registered as a freeholder in 1748, so the family must still have been of some importance in South Tynedale. There have been Armstrongs in Northumberland for centuries, as well as the Scottish branch who had their headquarters in Liddesdale, and who took part in the famous 'Fray of Hautwessel' near the end of the sixteenth century.

Ironically enough, it was due to Alec Ridley "who shot too well" that the Armstrongs were defeated! John took his wife to live on his holding at Ramshawrigg, which is south of the town of Haltwhistle on the vast expanse of Plenmellor Common. This is wild hill country and would be described today as marginal land. It was five years after 'The '45' when John and Anne went to Ramshawrigg, but there is no record that before this marriage John was in any way concerned in the second Jacobite Rebellion. The Ridleys had changed, and were now respectable yeomen, living comfortably—as heirlooms that still survive reveal. There would be very little tillage land at Ramshawrigg, John's time would be spent in stock-rearing and winning his hay crops in the summer. Little news would penetrate from the outside world to that remote corner of Northumberland, and to these Northumbrian farmers it would make little difference whether Stuarts or Hanoverians were on the throne of their country. Families came first in those days, and the most exciting events would be the births and marriages of their children. John and Anne had one son, Thomas, who, like his forebears, was baptized at Haltwhistle. It was in 1755 that this event took place, and twenty-two years later his marriage to Ann Pratt joins the many entries concerning the Ridleys in the church registers of Haltwhistle. Ann Pratt is described as being of Haltwhistle Parish, but, as I have already mentioned, the parish included Bardon Mill at that time.

Thomas's bride was most likely one of the Bardon Mill Pratts a family which until not long ago still lived in the district. Thomas was more enterprising than his forebears and took his bride across the border into the neighbouring county of Cumberland. Quite something for the stay-at-home Ridleys. Their new home was 'Ye Banks' near the river Irthing between Gilsland and Brampton, and not far from the ruins of the beautiful Lanercost Priory. Evidently no Ridley could endure exile from his county for long, and Thomas and Ann crossed the border again to live at Birkshaw north of Bardon Mill, which was a small fortified pele house.

Here in 1791 was born my great-grandfather Matthew Ridley, and in the same year, conforming to tradition, he was taken to Haltwhistle Church for his christening. My father always swore that he could remember his grandfather, but, though I hate to cast doubts on the veracity of one whom I so dearly loved, I am afraid it is one of those family stories. On the tombstone in Beltingham churchyard, the inscription to the memory of my great-grand-parents and three of their children reads that Matthew Ridley was born in the year 1791 and died in 1870. Like many children who listen to 'tales of a grandfather' the children really believe that they themselves were alive at the time. Great-grand-father Matthew's life spanned four reigns, 'Farmer' George, as George III liked to call himself, was on the throne when he was born; the Prince Regent became king in 1820; in 1830 William IV followed his brother; and in 1837 began the longest reign in our history when Matthew Ridley was a man of 46. Victoria was queen, she who was to become the embodiment of the British way of life for more than sixty 'glorious years'.

This Matthew brought some romance into a somewhat dull and conventional family. He eloped! How many times have I listened to the story of great-grandfather's romance. In those days there was an inn, called 'The Water House', between Haydon Bridge and Bardon Mill. (Where is the picture now of this old-time port of call, that used to hang in the passage at Peel Well?) 'The Water House' was on the north side of the road, east of what was then a blacksmith's shop, and the foundations can still be traced. In William Lee's *Haydon Bridge and District* there are horrific tales of what went on at 'The Water House'. The rather wild young men of the district used to gather there and drink far into the night. Bets were laid and disasters followed. A Cowing of

Morley (Moralee on the ordnance map) was drowned in the Tyne "near The Water House" as late as 1852, while in 1849 another Cowing came to a violent end on his way from Halt-whistle to the notorious inn.

A sad and fatal accident occured at Melkridge, to Mr. Thomas Cowing, son of Mr. Matthew Cowing of High Morley. The deceased and Mr. Nicholas Maughan had been at Haltwhistle, and on leaving the latter place, on their return home, they tried the speed of their horses, dashing off at a furious rate, but they had not gone far, when the deceased's horse galloped against the end of a house occupied by Mr. Liddell, Melkridge, killing the rider on the spot.

Nicholas Maughan, who survived, lived at Newbrough, and a desk which he once owned, dating from about 1775 passed into the possession of 'young' Matthew Ridley and stands in the writer's home at Wylam today.

As a child I can remember going to the house at Melkridge where Liddells still lived, and as the gable end of the house jutted into the road a galloping horse would have no chance of avoiding it. Now a new road to Haltwhistle runs north of Melkridge, and very few people will remember the circumstances of Thomas Cowing's death.

With its bad reputation it is not surprising that the fathers of marriageable daughters did not look with a kindly eye on the young men who frequented 'The Water House'. One of these gentlemen lived in the square stone-built house of Whitechapel, which looks very much today as it would then. This gentleman, whose name was Woodman, had an exceedingly pretty daughter who attracted the attention of young Matthew Ridley as he rode past on his way from Birkshaw to join his cronies at 'The Water House'. I may say that this part of the story was not told to me as a child. I have found it out since. Certainly it makes for variety and brightens up the Ridleys. Jane's father became so disturbed by the frequent sight of Matthew riding past his house that he sent his daughter for safety to some Woodman relations at the farm of Grindon, which is a little way south of the Military Road and north of Haydon Bridge.

Jane and Matthew must already have been meeting secretly, in spite of all the precautions taken for her safety, for it was not long before the young farmer from Birkshaw made up his mind to rescue the girl who was to become his wife. It is the conventional story of the distressed maiden climbing out of an upper window and landing in her lover's arms; he of course had his horse waiting and she rode pillion behind her future bridegroom. I should have thought it would have been wiser to have walked and led the horse some way before galloping off and no doubt rousing the sleeping household, but that would not have been dramatic enough for the nineteenth century. The family legend is that as Matthew and Jane rode off to freedom and later, marriage, that my great-grandfather sang verses from "Logie O'Buchan" an old Scottish song:

> O think't nae lang lassie,
> Though I gan awa'
> O think't nae lang lassie
> Though I gan awa'
> For Summer is coming,
> Cold winter's awa'
> And I'll come back and see thee
> In spite of them a'.

Matthew and his 'Bonnie Jean', as he always called her, were duly married, and the wild young man settled down into a model husband and successful farmer. Birkshaw was soon too small for an ambitious man and Matthew moved into the adjoining parish of Haydon Bridge to farm the considerable holding of Peel Well, to which in the years to come his son and grandsons added the farms of Lipwood Well, High Lipwood and Middle Lipwood and the 'out-bye' farm of Seldom Seen.

Matthew and Jane had four sons—Robert, William, Matthew and John—and it was in giving birth to John that my great-grandmother died at the early age of 46. Her sampler, which she worked in 1811 when she was a small girl at Whitechapel, hangs in my sitting-room as I write. On the mantelpiece is a silver snuff box inscribed "W. Ridley 1876". This was my great Uncle William's ,who died when he was 56; while his brother Robert, born in 1818, died at the age of 49. Neither of them married. The baby, John, only survived his mother by five years. They are all buried in the churchyard at Beltingham, in the country from which they sprang.

The outstanding member of Jane and Matthew's family was their son, also a Matthew, who was my grandfather. He lived until just before the First World War, and one could rightly say he rampaged through life. Ruthless, ambitious, arrogant, how can I describe him? He had none of the gentle qualities attributed to both his parents, and certainly none of his own children that I remember resembled him in any way.

He conformed almost like a text book to the overbearing Victorian husband and father of fiction. That he was a first-class farmer and breeder of pedigree stock there is no question whatsoever, and the men who worked for him (some are still alive) have told me that he was a good and just master. It was in his family life that he displayed his less attractive qualities. My grandmother, who was Mary Charlton, is a shadowy figure, always referred to by her children as 'Mama'. She was a beautiful needlewoman, and I know my father loved her devotedly, but she died long before I was born—worn out by child-bearing, I should imagine. So overbearing was this Matthew Ridley that even when his children were adults his word was law. If he felt in the mood, I have been told, he would rouse the household at five o'clock in the morning to play cards with him, and none dared to disobey! He sent all his family to boarding schools, but when they returned they had to conform to his dictates. Neither of his sons wanted to be farmers, countrymen though they were. William, especially, had intellectual tendencies; he was kind and gentle, and loved by all who knew him. It was Uncle Billie, as I called him, who gave me my first doll's pram. He had been to The Dublin Horse Show with his brother-in-law, my godfather, Uncle George Pearson, and for me he brought this present, complete with a knitted emerald-green rug. Another present he gave me was a brooch in the form of two cat's heads which I called "my puffy-cat brooch". I can still remember my grief when I lost my 'puffy-cats' in a railway compartment at Ryton. My memories of Ryton have never been happy ones. This gentle man died of pneumonia when he was only 50.

Although his heart was never in farming, it was William's untiring work behind the scenes which made the Peel Well flock of Border Leicester sheep so famous, though it was Matthew Ridley who reaped all the glory. I have been told that my grandfather never did any manual work in his life; he was an administrator, who knew what should be done, but was careful to see that someone else did it for him. None of the Ridley men were what is known as typical farmers. (I doubt if any one is really typical of anything, but it is now an accepted term.) They were all extremely well read, interested in world affairs, and my father was keenly interested in history and politics. Anything less like the popular conception of the red-faced farmer flanked by a roaring bull is difficult to imagine.

My aunts were all sent as termly boarders to a school for 'young ladies' in Morpeth. There they produced exquisite needlework, some of which I still possess. One, Aunt Lydia, was an accomplished pianist, but their ventures into art were not so successful. I remember a ghastly water colour of an anaemic looking little girl gazing vacantly at a terrified canary! I loved to listen to the stories of what they did when they were at school. From what I remember the name of the headmistress was Mrs. Armstrong, and the school was in Wansbeck House—this would subsequently become Morpeth High School for Girls, at which I presented the prizes in 1966. In summer the boarders used to walk from Morpeth by the side of the Wansbeck to church at Mitford. My Aunt Jane (The girl in the picture) went back to her old school as a member of the staff. Jane Ridley was engaged to be married when she died suddenly. The cause of her untimely death was always referred to as "the pain in Janie's side". Possibly it was appendicitis, as she was the oldest of the family and it was not until the illness of Edward VII—which resulted in the postponement of his coronation—that operations were performed for 'a pain in the side'.

It is said that we cannot escape from our past, and I certainly am a firm believer in heredity. Not one of my forebears, with the exception of Thomas Ridley, who 'emigrated' to Cumberland for a short time, has ever lived beyond the boundaries of his own county. I cannot picture myself living anywhere else but in Northumberland. I should feel alien and homesick for the land of my birth.

When I was a child I loved my county, and as I have grown older the love has strengthened. My early life was supremely happy, secure in the love of my parents, surrounded by animals which I adored and still do. I see my father riding into the yard on Scottie, followed by Moss, a sheep dog, who was succeeded by Sweep, and my father telling me the most wonderful stories about the entirely imaginary adventures of the dogs, horses and cats which I absolutely believed. I must have been a most gullible child! I don't think my father ever liked sending cattle or sheep to the fat-stock markets, and for a long time I thought they had only gone on holiday. I loved my home, and though I have never been inside the house since I left it long ago, I can picture every room as it used to be. It was so warm and cosy, although we had only oil-lamps and none of the labour-saving gadgets of today—though we were thought to be very grand because we had a bathroom. My mother was a most wonderful woman, and the greatest compliment I can pay to her is that I would have chosen her to be my mother had I been given the choice. She was intensely practical and far ahead of the times. I think the only bone of contention in those days was my tendency to break into broad Northumbrian. Every effort was made to stop me and to break off this dreadful habit, but it was of no avail, and today I am bilingual.

Little did I ever think that in the years ahead I would become associated with a study of the Northumbrian speech or that it would contribute towards my livelihood.

This then is the story of a very ordinary family, but a family to which I am proud to belong. None of us has had a distinguished career, none of us will leave any mark on history, but each in his own way has lived his life according to his lights. Of my father I would say he served his day and generation well, in so much that he was a good and considerate master; he was generous to a fault, and through his long years of ill-health I can never remember hearing him complain. He was the most wonderful mimic and had a glorious sense of humour which never failed him. His name for me was Thomas. I am sure both he and my mother must have grieved greatly for the son who died in infancy, but never once did they make me feel I was 'only a girl'. When my father died his coffin was taken to his resting place in one of his own 'long' carts drawn by one of his horses, and six of his own men laid him in his grave.

Much has happened to me since those long ago days at Lipwood Well, and through the years—some of which I confess have been anything but happy—I have been sustained by the knowledge that none of my forebears ever gave up. To them all I owe a debt of gratitude.

This line of Ridleys from the reign of William and Mary to

Elizabeth II ends with me, but the name will never die out as long as Northumberland exists.

If in any way I have made these ordinary people come to life then I have achieved my object. Some have been better than others, all have had their failings as well as their virtues, which makes them all the more lovable. I am ending this chapter with a perfectly true story about my grandfather, who, in spite of his domineering ways, I am told was always himself and couldn't stand people who tried to be other than what they were.

The old man was asked to propose a toast at the Border Union Show Dinner at Kelso, a dinner which was held in 'The Cross Keys'. I have stood in the room where Matthew Ridley made surely the shortest speech on record. He had become very tired of all the flattery and compliments paid by the previous speakers so that by the time his turn came, he was not only nauseated by the hypocrisy but had been doing justice to the whisky of which he was very fond. Staggering to his feet, he looked round the table, and then breaking into broadest Northumbrian, he said,

"Mr. Chairman, me Lords and gentlemen, there've been plenty of lies tell't without me telling any mair" ... and sat down.

2

A DAY OF DISCOVERY:
Old Bewick and Ros Castle

I will lift up mine eyes unto the hills:
From whence cometh my help.

Psalm 121

Sometimes people say to me, "You must know every inch of Northumberland"; and my reply is that Northumberland is so vast, so varied in its scenery and historic buildings, that not even a lifetime's research could ever merit such an exaggerated statement. I realize only too well how much I have still to see and learn about my beloved county.

On a July day during the glorious summer of 1969 I set out from my home at Wylam in Tynedale with two friends to explore some of the places about which I had heard so much and yet had never had the opportunity to visit. It is a most exciting feeling to find new places in the county of one's birth, and 17th July was not only a day of discovery, but a day to remember. The first part of the journey was along the familiar roads which lead to Rothbury, the capital of Coquetdale. The streets of Rothbury were, to use a Northumbrian word, 'hotchin' (alive) with visitors, many no doubt on their way to see the justly famous grounds of Lord Armstrong's home at Cragside, while the walkers and climbers wended their way towards the Simonside Range of hills. We took the road from Rothbury to Powburn, where we crossed the Devil's Causeway on our way to Eglingham. The hedgerows were ablaze with wild roses and the flowers in the cottage gardens were a riot of colour in the sleepy little village. Our original idea was to make for Chillingham, but as we passed a road end a little way beyond the hamlet of Old Bewick we saw a Celtic cross standing at the road end. Immediately curiosity was roused, and we bundled out of the car to investigate. On the base of the cross, on the side away from the road we deciphered the following inscription; "To the glory of God in loving memory of John Charles Langlands. 1874." Then on a notice board we read "Chapel of The Holy Trinity", and I suddenly realized that we had found the road to Old Bewick church, about which I had heard so much but had never had the opportunity to visit. Until I entered this remote church I had always maintained that the most beautiful church in all Northumberland was at Beltingham in South Tynedale. Now, however, St. Cuthbert's at Beltingham has a rival place in my affections in the Chapel of The Holy Trinity at Old Bewick. Every church, at least to me, has a different atmosphere; some are sombre and awe inspiring, some are happy and gay, and Old Bewick is one of the latter. As you open the door the feeling of happiness greets you, as though the church was saying, "My foundations have survived the centuries, and the ceaseless Border warfare, and like the inscription on the Celtic cross, I stand here to the glory of God."

The church stands on gently rising ground on the sunny side of a small stream appropriately named the Kirk Burn. The churchyard is surrounded by trees, overlooked by the bracken-clad Bewick Hill, which rises to a height of 773 feet above sea level. A mass of sandstone, which projects from Bewick Hill, is known as the 'Hanging Crag', and an old couplet says:

> As long as the Hanging Crag shall stand
> There'll aye be a Ha' on Bewick land.

Judging from the names on headstones in the churchyard, the family of Hall is still prominent in the district. On the summit of Bewick Hill is a perfect specimen of a Celtic hill-fortress, where long ago the tribes from the Breamish Valley took refuge in times of danger. Wild and dangerous was this part of Northumberland, and bloody is its history. Like many other Northumbrian churches, Holy Trinity has lain in ruins and has twice been restored since it was built in the twelfth century.

It is possible that the original church is of an even earlier period, as in Volume XIV of *The County History*, attention is drawn to the fact that the capitals on the chancel arch were obviously done by the same hands as the capitals in the Norman chapel at Durham Castle, that is before or about 1105.

Jane Ridley, Victorian schoolgirl

The writer's mother in her 'smart' turn-out

The Northumberland coast from the summit of Ros Castle

It was about this time that Queen Maud, a daughter of St. Margaret of Scotland, gave the manor of Bewick to Tynemouth Priory and at the same time restored the church at Old Bewick. Maud, or Matilda as she is sometimes called, became the wife of Henry I of England, and the effigy in Holy Trinity is sometimes mistakenly described as that of the queen. This is most unlikely, as the effigy, now much defaced, dates from the early thirteenth century. No doubt this statement of mine will arouse controversy, as the local people are determined to have the effigy of a queen of England in their church! It is impossible to convince Northumbrians that they may be wrong, once they have made up their minds that they are right; a Northumbrian is 'never wrang'. The unknown lady's head lies on a cushion between two kneeling angels under a trefoiled and crocketed canopy, and is covered with a fillet-bound handkerchief. Her dress is a tight-waisted kirtle with buttoned sleeves, and a mantle with long lappets. Her feet in pointed shoes rest on a crouching lion. It is thought to be the work of sculptors who had a workshop in or near Alnwick from the thirteenth century until about 1340. Northumbrian churches are singularly lacking in sculpture or effigies, due no doubt to the hundreds of years of warfare, when Northumberland was the buffer-state between two countries.

In 1253 Old Bewick had a market established by Henry III, and during the last century part of the market cross was discovered in a field not far from where the memorial to Mr. Langlands stand today. The architectural details of Holy Trinity fail to convey how beautiful this gem of Northumbrian churches is, so small, yet so impressive. Possibly it is the procession of Norman arch followed by Norman apse that make this essentially Norman building so dramatic. One small original window remains in the nave, and there is an even smaller one in the chancel. (The whole building is composed of nave and chancel only.)

It is amazing that the church withstood the ravages of time and warfare until the seventeenth century when that despoiler of beauty, Cromwell, was at large in Northumberland. (The Roundhead leader is said to have stayed at the not far-distant Eglingham Hall.) A great deal of damage was done to Holy Trinity by Cromwellian soldiers under the command of General Leslie. (There is no evidence that horses were stabled there in the days of the Civil Wars as they were in Durham Cathedral.)

3

This wanton destruction was repaired by the then Lord of the Manor, Ralph Williamson, in 1695. The restored building weathered the storms, until the late eighteenth century, when a mighty gale which swept the district blew off the roof. The church lay in ruins until 1866, when another restoration, of which Mr. J. C. Langlands was a benefactor, began. A memorial tablet in the church commemorates his generosity and bears the inscription: "I was glad when they said unto me we will go into the house of the Lord." There are three brass tablets to the memory of young men killed in the wars, two of these bearing the name of Langlands. Holy Trinity is a remarkable restoration for Victorian times, as so much of the original Norman and Decorated work has been preserved, and not replaced by pseudo-Gothic. In 1850 some sanctuary bells were discovered, and they can be seen in the vestry today. There is also a well-preserved holy-water stoup.

If one can describe a churchyard as a happy place, then that of Old Bewick certainly is. The grass is cut, the paths well kept, and there are bunches of flowers on the graves. One headstone is surmounted by the eagle of The Royal Air Force. It is to the memory of a young man of 20. If ever there is a competition for the best-kept church and surroundings, on the same lines as the best-kept village competition, then Old Bewick should be well at the top of the list. It was with feelings of the greatest regret that at last we closed the church door. So sorry was I to say goodbye to the church among the trees that I turned back for one last look inside. There was the same feeling of joy and happiness that had been so strong when I first went in, and I felt that a voice was saying, "I am so glad you have come, come again." I have vowed that one day I will go back to this church I discovered purely by chance. Sad though it was to say farewell, I was glad that it had been my good fortune to find this jewel among Northumbrian churches. The presence of God is so real in the Church of the Holy Trinity that one feels miracles could still be performed within its walls and an unbeliever converted. I have been groping for a word that could comprehensively convey the atmosphere of this unique church, and the appropriate word is comfort. In this country of Till and Breamish, where scores of Cheviot sheep graze, two verses of a well-known hymn express so vividly the spirit of this little-known and unsung church of God.

Perverse and foolish oft I strayed,
And yet in love he sought me;
And on his shoulder gently laid,
And home, rejoicing brought me.

In death's dark vale I fear no ill
With thee, dear Lord beside me;
Thy rod and staff my comfort still,
Thy Cross before to guide me.

Elated by our discovery, we decided to go to Chillingham, only a few miles to the north of Old Bewick. When Chillingham is mentioned the immediate reaction is to think of the herd of Wild White Cattle, which is known all over the world. We had all seen the herd, and I had been to Chillingham church on several occasions, but not since the so-called improvements had been carried out. I am sorry to say that after the beauty and simplicity of Old Bewick, the church of St. Peter was something of a disappointment. In fact I cannot reconcile the description of the church which appears in the guide, with St. Peter's as it is today.

The visit to Chillingham church was the only disappointment we had on our day of discovery. I wish in some ways that I had not seen the alterations and kept my memories of the church as it was before. The wonderfully carved tomb of Sir Ralph Grey and his wife Elizabeth which dates from the mid-fifteenth century looks strangely lost and lonely in its depleted surroundings.

St. Peter's church was founded in the thirteenth century, and within the modern porch is a Norman doorway. The nave and chancel are also Norman. When that has been said there is very little to recommend the church as it is today. I admit that something had to be done to eradicate the dry rot which was discovered, but was it necessary to remove the south transept screen? The altar table of Doddington stone would not look out of place in an entirely modern building, but seems wrong in a Norman church. A great deal of blame has been attached to the Victorians for their unfortunate restorations; one wonders what future generations will have to say about some of the twentieth-century innovations.

Comparisons are said to be odious, but the contrast between the churchyards at Old Bewick and Chillingham is so marked that it is impossible not to make some comment. I realize Chillingham has a much more difficult problem as the land rises steeply to the church and beyond and the grass cannot be easy to cut, but little attempt seemed to have been made, at least in July, to tidy up the churchyard. In 1955 the parishes of Chillingham and Chatton were united, and are within the Rural Deanery of Bamburgh with Glendale, in the Lindisfarne Archdeaconry of the Newcastle Diocese.

The vicar in his address of welcome expresses the hope that those who come to his church will leave with a feeling of spiritual refreshment, now and in the years to come. I hope that with some visitors these wishes have been fulfilled. I do agree with the vicar when he says that during the years of restoration there was dust and controversy. This I can well believe!

Chillingham had been an anti-climax, but our next 'ploy' was not (this most expressive Scottish word describes exactly what we were doing; the literal translation is employment, a harmless frolic, a merry meeting). Our introduction to Ros Castle was indeed a merry meeting. The road follows the wall of Chillingham Park for a time, and then a minor road turns to the left. This gated road climbs steadily, passing close to the farm of Hebburn, or Hepburn—the Scottish form is used on the ordnance map. The local pronunciation is Hebron. The Northumbrian has an amazing capacity for mispronunciation, and will 'Northumbrianize' any word to suit his fancy. The township of Hebburn forms the southern part of Chillingham parish, with our friend Old Bewick in Eglingham parish in the south. It was in 1293 that the boundary was set out, and remains very much the same today. Hebburn Wood is still the boundary between Hebburn and Old Bewick, though the many little streams which flow through it are no longer part of the boundaries of the two parishes. The district is still well wooded, as it was long ago when Nicholas of Hebburn gave the priest of St. Mary's chapel wild honey and wax from the trees. At one time there was a family of Hebburn, who, like many others, took their surname from their dwelling. The coat of arms of this family is of interesting origin: "argent three cressets sables flaming proper", said to be taken from the beacon on Ros Castle.

At Hebburn is a roofless bastle-house (a fortified dwelling peculiar to this Border country), said to be one of the most interesting pieces of domestic architecture in the district. The last of the Hebburn family, Robert, died in 1755, and nothing has been done to the tower since. The tower is mentioned in a survey of 1514 (the year after Flodden), again in 1541 and in 1654. It was then referred to as a 'mansion house', and was considerably larger than the existing bastle-house.

Robert Hebburn's daughter and heiress went to live with her mother's relations in the south after her father's death. This heiress married the Reverend Edward Brudenell, who is said to have pulled down most of the old 'mansion house' of his wife's ancestors, and built a small shooting lodge, which may be the house now known as Hebburn Bell. Some historians feel that Hebburn's bastle-house should be re-roofed, and preserved as a typical fortified house of its time. The name Hebburn is thought to be derived from the old English word Hehburh meaning a fortress, and this name may originally have been applied to what is now Ros Castle. The name appears as Hepburn in the ballad of Lord Hepburn by Sheldon, in his *Minstrelsy of the English Border*. There is a legend that near the house of Hebburn Bell the Dissenters used to meet in secret before the passing of the Toleration Act in 1688, the year of the 'Glorious Revolution'.

As we left Hebburn and its bastle-house behind, the road started to rise steeply, and looking back there was the most wonderful view of the Cheviot Range. Already my Northumbrian blood was stirred by the beauty of my county, and I thought of the verse of Scott's poem, hackneyed though it may be:

> Breathes there a man with soul so dead,
> Who never to himself hath said,
> This is my own, my native land.

As I got out to open the last gate a stiff breeze was blowing, one of "the winds from off the sea" which one rarely escapes in Northumberland. We left the car by the roadside; there were only two other cars near us. How different from the well-known beauty spots of the South and West Country, where cars are parked bumper to bumper.

I had often heard how wonderful the prospect from Ros Castle was, but in my wildest dreams I had never visualized how truly magnificent the reality would be. The disappointment of Chillingham Church was forgotten, the view from the summit was to rank with the joy of discovering Old Bewick. The climb from the road to the summit is short but almost sheer as the end is in sight. We had been advised to follow the dry-stone wall, and this sound advice we took. Loose stones and rubble added to the hazards, and we scrambled like mountain goats, with heads down until at last we were there. Another ambition of mine was realized. I was standing on the summit of Ros Castle, 1036 feet above sea level, with Northumberland spread out like an aerial photograph before me. Ros Castle is the highest point in the chain of high ground known as the Kyloe Hills—part of the Great Whin Sill of Northumberland—which rise near Belford and end at Ros Castle.

In prehistoric times there was a double-ramparted earthwork on this highest point of the Kyloes, and the remains of it are still visible. In the days of perpetual warfare beacons flared from the summit. No doubt the fires were lit when England was threatened with invasion from Spain, and in the days when Napoleon's invasion was expected at any time, Ros Castle's beacon gave the warning. There is an amusing account in David Dippie Dixon's book *The Vale of Whittingham* of the false alarm of 1804 when the fear of 'Boney' was strong. Some of the gentry had their arsenals at the ready to repel the upstart emperor.

During the scare the beacon was lit on Ros Castle. The flames warned the watchers in Coquetdale and Alndale, but the spirit of the Border raiders seemed to have departed, many of the local men had peculiar excuses for staying at home. One, Tom Bolam, had a pain in his "breest" and needed three glasses of whisky to cure it. Willie Middlehams had a "bad" pain, and Jack Dixon's horse needed shoeing. It was rather odd that when the alarm proved to be false, all these gentlemen were well enough to go to a thanksgiving dinner at Collingwood House at Cornhill!

Descendants of these men had no pains in their 'breests' 136 years later, when, as members of the Home Guard, they scanned the coastline for the coming of Hitler's forces. There could be no better vantage point in Northumberland than Ros Castle. Mile upon mile of the county rolls away to the sea, with Cheviot standing guardian in the south-west. Now people climb to where the danger signals once flared, and there is a cairn to which every visitor must add a stone.

This view from the summit was a favourite one of a great Northumbrian, Grey of Fallodon, and there is now a stone bearing the following inscription.

Ros Castle Camp
This height with its wide prospect was a
favourite resort of Sir Edward Grey
Afterwards Viscount Grey of Fallodon. K.G.
Foreign Secretary, December 1905–December 1916.
In 1936 it was presented to The National Trust
as part of a Northumbrian memorial to him.

It is possible, if one knows where to look, to see Fallodon, set among trees, a mile and a half inland from Embleton Bay. Even after Grey became totally blind he used to be helped to the summit, where the view was described to him.

How can I express in words that glorious stretch of land and sea visible for so many miles. One thing is certain—its breathtaking beauty could never be exaggerated. In July the colouring was so vivid; the green of the bracken was darker than the grassy hills rolling down to the golden sands of Northumberland's incomparable coastline, while the North Sea was as blue as the Mediterranean. From the heights of the Kyloe Hills stretched the coastal plain, intersected by many roads, where the windscreens of the cars reflected the sunshine.

The fields of this great farming country were stocked with feeding cattle, while on the hills, the Cheviots and the 'half-breds' of Northumberland grazed. Far out to sea the Longstone Lighthouse was conspicuous, and the waves were breaking on the shores of The Farnes. From this height seven of Northumberland's many castles can be counted, those mighty fortresses which are some of the county's greatest treasures. Far away on the Holy Island of Lindisfarne, the fairy-tale castle of Lutyens and the ruins of the Priory could be easily picked out.

Lindisfarne is to Northumberland what Iona is to Scotland, and it was from the Holy Island that the missionaries went over to convert the heathen Northumbrians in the days when Northumbria was a kingdom that stretched from the Humber to the Forth. This island, which was the cradle of Christianity, should surely be regarded as sacrosanct; but in this restless age nothing however sacred is safe, and it was with horror that I read a report in a local newspaper that a scheme had been mooted to promote leisure centres and bingo on the island of the saints. Mercifully this revolting plan has been turned down by the area planning officer and the Public Health Committee of Norham and Islandshire's

Rural Council. The worst aspect of the affair was that some of the islanders were in favour of commercializing this hitherto unspoilt island. In the words of the local press,

> To allow an amusement arcade on Holy Island would be like inviting the money-changers who angered Jesus to go back into the temple. In spite of its attractions as a holiday centre, the island has managed to preserve much of the mystery and sanctity which gives it such remarkable character. It would be sacrilege to let this haven be invaded by prize bingo and shooting ranges.

Sentiments which I heartily endorse.

There are, however, many islanders who respect and love their heritage, and at the present time fourteen women are sewing a carpet for the island's church. The pattern is appropriately taken from illustrated Lindisfarne Gospels, and when the carpet is completed each contributor will have accomplished the enormous amount of 995,328 stitches. Truly a labour of love.

Away to the north the jagged tower of Haggerston can be discerned, while southwards rear the ruined towers of Dunstanburgh which are unmistakable. Between these two strongholds sprawls the mighty mass of Bamburgh, the rock on which it is built washed by the North Sea.

The Duke of Northumberland's home, Alnwick, is not so easy to distinguish; binoculars and a map are necessary to pin-point the 'Windsor of the North'. Chillingham, of course, is easy to find; it is so close to the heights which guard it. Once the property of the Greys, and now owned by the Earl of Tankerville, the castle is no longer occupied, although the earl and his family still live on the estate. Some people think Chillingham is one of the most picturesque of Northumbrian castles.

The last of the seven castles discernible from Ros Castle is Ford, the castle where King Jamie spent his last night before meeting his death on Flodden Field. The property of Lord Joicey, Ford is now used for educational courses by Northumberland County Council.

This is a very inadequate attempt to paint in words the glory of Northumberland as seen from the heights of the Great Whin Sill, and to inform the reader of what to expect when Ros Castle is ascended for the first time. If I know anything of my fellow Northumbrians, arguments will break out about the identity of the seven castles; it could not be otherwise. It will be interesting to see how many other contenders there are for the 'castle stakes'.

On that July day of unforgettable memory we met on the summit a couple from London who had never been in Northumberland before. They were incredulous that so much grandeur existed in a county which they had imagined was a mass of pit-heaps and factory chimneys. They could scarcely believe that there was not a sign of industry to be seen in all that vast expanse of country. As they extolled the beauties of my county I felt prouder than ever to be Northumbrian born and bred. It was with great reluctance that we began the descent to the road; a wonderful day was coming to an end, but a day that would be one of the red-letter days of 1969. It was almost too much to assimilate in one day, Old Bewick and Ros Castle, two of Northumberland's gems added to the county's necklace of precious stones. At last we tore ourselves away and came back to earth, returning home by way of Alnwick, where we drank a toast to Northumberland in 'The White Swan'. Leaving Alnwick by way of the Great North Road, we cut across country at Morpeth and eventually reached home at "Canny Wylam on the Tyne".

I am writing this on a wild November night, the wind is blowing gale force, and the rain is beating against the window; yet I have been hardly aware of the storm outside so immersed have I been in my day of discovery. It will be fearsome on the heights of Ros Castle tonight, yet with the dawn of another day, the view will emerge, not as it was in July, but magnificent still in its wildness. Far away on the coast the North Sea will be dashing against the rocks, and the mighty castles standing guard as they have done throughout the centuries. Soon the cattle will be brought 'inside', only the hardy outliers will weather the long northern winter outside, and the stockmen and shepherds of Northumberland will stand guard over their charges as the castles do over the coastline.

Our day of discovery will remain green in our memories, though Ros Castle may be covered with snow and the church at Old Bewick wait lonely and deserted for the coming of summer.

The great joy of a county such as Northumberland is that there are so many days of discovery to look forward to, the supply is never ending. There is always a tomorrow in Northumberland.

3

Josephine Butler, Nineteenth-century Crusader

And now abideth faith, hope, charity, these three;
but the greatest of these is charity.

I Corinthians 13:13

A name which should be emblazoned on Northumberland's scroll of fame is that of Josephine Butler, born Josephine Grey.

At the time of her 'Great Crusade' her name was internationally known, but sadly with the passing of the years, she is almost forgotten even in her native county of Northumberland. I have, while collecting material for this chapter, been disappointed to meet so many people who have never heard of this courageous and compassionate woman. The reason for this lack of knowledge may have something to do with the kind of work she did.

Her 'Great Crusade', as she herself called it, was an endeavour to repeal the Vice Regulations, also known as the Contagious Diseases Act; in other words she championed an unpopular cause that of the reform of the harsh laws operating in the nineteenth-century regarding prostitutes and prostitution. Even in the so-called permissive society of today, it is amazing how many people fight shy of the subject, and refer to Josephine Butler—if they have heard of her—as a social reformer, without mentioning the kind of reform in which she was so passionately engaged.

This woman, who has been described as the most heroic and the most sympathetic figure of the nineteenth century, ranks with Florence Nightingale and Elizabeth Fry; yet while their names are still household words, that of Josephine Butler is not given the recognition her work deserves. To nurse as Florence Nightingale did, to visit prisons like Elizabeth Fry, was respectable; whereas Josephine Butler's campaign was unmentionable. Yet her courage to involve herself in this unsavoury cause was immeasurably greater than that of the other women pioneers of that time.

Not for one moment do I wish to minimize the great work which Florence Nightingale and Elizabeth Fry did, but they were not facing to the same extent the social ostracism which Josephine Butler endured so bravely.

In the Lady Chapel of Liverpool Cathedral is a stained glass window depicting twenty-one noble women. Two of these heroines are Northumbrians, Josephine Butler and Grace Darling. The difference between these two women is that the first chose the path which led her to immortality, while the second had greatness thrust upon her and rose to the occasion like the brave woman she was. It has been suggested to me that another reason for the eclipse of Josephine Butler may be because hers is a story one cannot tell to children, while that of Grace Darling is such a typical example of heroism that has been told to generations of children far beyond the boundaries of Northumberland. I think there is a great deal of truth in this theory, for I remember as a child hearing the story of Grace Darling until I knew it almost by heart. In Grandfather Ridley's house there was a huge picture which I admired enormously of Grace and her father rowing their coble on their voyage to rescue the survivors of *The Forfarshire*.

When I asked who Josephine Butler was—after seeing her portrayed in 'The Pageant of Noble Women', which was held in Haydon Bridge Town Hall—I was told that "she was a lady who did good work". There was also at Peel Well a print of Josephine's father, John Grey, who was at one time agent for the Greenwich Hospital Estate, by which Peel Well was then owned.

My object in writing this chapter is, if possible, to revive the memory of Josephine Butler in her own county, and to give her name the place it so richly deserves in the annals of Northumberland.

It has been my great good fortune to meet and talk with a grand-daughter of Mrs. Butler's. This is Miss Hetha Butler of Wooler, who has given me help and information regarding 'Grannie', as she refers to this champion of justice. Talking to Miss Butler, and listening to her memories of 'Grannie' has brought Josephine Butler alive and made her something more than a "lady who did good works". I am greatly indebted to Miss

Butler for her help and the insight she has given me into 'Grannie's' character.

In the picture of Josephine Butler reproduced in this book, the expression of her face is that of serenity and compassion, and I quote an extract from a letter to me from her grand-daughter: "When you said she looked compassionate, I think you struck the keynote of her character. She was indeed compassionate, and her great compassion for the poor girls who suffered so cruelly under the C.D. Acts compelled her to go forward." The C.D. Act referred to by Miss Butler was the Contagious Diseases Act, which Josephine Butler felt to be extremely unjust and strongly biased in favour of men.

The future reformer was born in 1828 at Milfield near Wooler. Milfield is a village on the road from Wooler to Cornhill, and is set in the heart of Glendale, which is Cheviot country. The plain on which Milfield lies has a background of the range of these hills which form part of the border between England and Scotland. Through the plain meanders the river Till on its way to join the Tweed at Tillmouth, close to Twizel Bridge over which Surrey led his artillery on the way to Flodden. Within the bounds of Glendale is some of the most historic and beautiful scenery in the county, unmarred today by any sign of industry. The house in which Josephine Grey was born has been demolished and a new house built in its place.

The Greys are an old Northumbrian family, with three main branches, those of Howick, Fallodon and Milfield, and it was to the latter branch that Josephine's father John Grey belonged. In 1815 John Grey married Hannah Annett of Alnwick, whose family had originally been Huguenot refugees. They had a family of nine children, three boys and six girls, Josephine being the seventh of the large family. John Grey was a noted agriculturist with ideas and views far ahead of his times. He was a man of wide interests and intellectual ability. In some ways John Grey was of a reforming inclination and interested himself in the social and political affairs of the times, so that from an early age his children were aware of the outside world.

The first six years of Josephines' life were spent at Milfield, in the secure atmosphere of a loving and devoted family. She was extremely devoted to her sister Harriet, a devotion which lasted until Harriet's death, when her sister wrote an appreciation in the form which she described as "In Memoriam; Harriet Meuricoffre, By her sister, Josephine Butler." In spite of the fact that Harriet's married life was spent abroad, the bond between the sisters was never broken.

In 1834 The Commissioners of The Greenwich Hospital appointed John Grey as Receiver or Agent for their estates at Dilston in Tynedale.

These estates were sequestrated to the Crown after the execution of the third Earl of Derwentwater in 1716 and were administered by the Greenwich Hospital. The year after his appointment as Greenwich Hospital Agent John Grey and his family went to live at Dilston, and here, amid romantic surroundings, Josephine Grey grew up. John Grey was to live there for many years, and was succeeded as agent by his son, Charles, until the estates were sold and became the property of the Beaumont family, the head of which is the present Lord Allendale.

How delighted Josephine Grey would be to know that the Hall at Dilston has now become a home for handicapped children. What an appropriate gesture it would be if her name could be commemorated in some way when the Hall begins its new phase.

The Grey family spent their young days in two of the most lovely parts of Northumberland, Glendale and the romantic Dilston. As children they no doubt played by the side of the Devil's Water, and scrambled about the ruins of Dilston Castle—of which only the gatehouse remains. (In spite of many precautions taken by Lord Allendale, vandals have done their best to wreck what remains of the old tower of the Radcliffes.) When the Greys were at Dilston the decapitated body of "Derwentwater's bonnie martyred Earl" still lay in the chapel; it was not until 1874 that the remains were taken for re-interment at Thorndon in Essex. The Grey children must often have listened to the Derwentwater Story.

In her book on her sister Harriet, Josephine Butler tells us something of her education:

Living in the country, far from any town, and, if I may say so, in the pre-educational era (for women at least) we had none of the advantages which girls of the present day have. But we owed much to our dear mother who was very firm in requiring from us that whatever we did should be thoroughly done, and in taking up any study we should aim at becoming as perfect as we could in it, without external aid. This was a moral discipline which perhaps compensated in value for the lack of a great store of knowledge. She would assemble us daily for the reading aloud of some solid book, and by a kind of examination following the reading, assure herself that we had mastered the subject. She urged us to aim at excellence, if not perfection, in at least one thing. Our father's connection with great public movements of the day,—the first Reform Bill, the Abolition of the Slave Trade and Slavery, and the Free Trade movement, gave us a very early interest in public questions, and in the history of our country.

For two years my sister and I were together at a school in Newcastle.

Miss Hetha Butler has added a postscript to this and says, "When at Dilston they did have a governess (a strict one). . . . Aunt Harriet said in one of her letters that Josephine was so good and patient at explaining difficulties to others which never troubled her own clever head." This then was the kind of world in which Josephine Grey grew up. The life of a well brought-up young lady of the times.

She was taught to paint in water colours; I have seen two of her pictures at Miss Butler's home. She was an accomplished musician, and in years to come her admirers presented her with a rosewood grand piano by Broadwood. This instrument was awarded a prize at the Great Exhibition of 1851 at the Crystal Palace, and Jennie Lind, 'The Swedish Nightingale', sang to its accompaniment, with Sterndale Bennett at the piano. Josephine was for a time a pupil of Sterndale Bennett. The piano was at Ewart near Wooler until 1937.

One of the many endearing characteristics of Josephine Grey was her profound love of animals, and a verse of a hymn epitomizes her attitude towards all God's creatures.

> Each little flower that opens,
> Each little bird that sings,
> He made their glowing colours,
> He made their tiny wings.

The Grey girls were all good horsewomen, and in their youth they hunted regularly. I had heard a story to the effect that a favourite pony which Josephine had loved dearly was buried in the wood at Dilston and the place marked with a stone slab. Due to the kindness of Lord Allendale's Agent, Mr. Fogget, and the Head Forester, Mr. Shipp, I verified this story in the summer of 1969. Close to where the saw-mill is now at Dilston is the grave of the pony, Apple, and on the gravestone is the following inscription:

> "In Memoriam Apple.
> Aged 28 years 18—"

(time has obliterated the rest of the date.) In one of Josephine's letters she mentions the death of Apple, which was probably some time before her marriage. Close beside the grave of Apple is another gravestone to the memory of a dog, but as the date on it is clearly 1899 it cannot have belonged to the Greys, perhaps it was the well-loved dog of one of the Beaumonts, the then owners of Dilton. This inscription reads:

> "In Memoriam, Portos O.B.
> August 14 1899. Fidus ad Extremum."

This love of animals remained with Josephine all her life, and she was violently opposed to vivisection.

There was nothing of the blue stocking about the future crusader. She loved parties and balls, and there is an account of her attending a very grand Hunt Ball at Alnwick Castle, wearing real flowers in her hair. As is to be expected, she had many admirers, but until she met George Butler, she does not seem to have been very interested in the young men she met. Miss Butler recounts the following anecdote;

> I heard a story of Grannie before she was married when she was at Dilston and lots of young people were wont to stay there. One day as she walked in the woods a stick caught in the hem of her long gown and was dragged along as she walked. A young man of the party coming behind her said, "You have a follower Miss Grey." At once and without looking round she answered, "All my followers are sticks."

One cannot help feeling sorry for the young man. It was in 1850 when she was 22 that she met the man she did not dismiss as a stick, this was George Butler who was a lecturer at the University of Durham. George Butler was one of a highly gifted and intellectual family. Both his father and brother were headmasters of Harrow, his brother being the youngest head ever appointed at that famous school. Like many clever people George Butler was inclined to be lazy, and wasted much time when at Oxford. He left the city of dreaming spires for Cambridge, where he obtained his degree, and later in life returned to Oxford as public examiner. Josephine in her widowhood wrote *Recollections of George Butler, by his wife.*

In 1851, Josephine made a journey to London to see the Great Exhibition. In the same year she became engaged, and her life at Dilston was coming to an end. Josephine Grey and George Butler were married in January of 1852 in the ancient parish church of St. Andrews at Corbridge on the Tyne. She must have made a charming bride, as all who knew her emphasize how attractive and feminine she was, the exact opposite of the popular idea of a social reformer. Until old age, Josephine Butler, as she now was, spent most of her life far away from Northumberland, only occasionally coming north to visit relations or to crusade for her cause. Yet through all those long and arduous years she never lost her love for her own county.

The newly married couple set up house in Oxford, where later George Butler was ordained. It was while at Oxford that Josephine's social conscience was roused. I can find no record of how she first became interested in the unmentionable problem of prostitution. She does often say in her letters and in her book *Personal Reminiscences of a Great Crusade* that she was often sickened by the indifference of the upper classes to the squalor and vice which existed. The Victorians were experts in the use of blinkers when it came to anything unpleasant or 'not quite nice'. Ladies, of course, were not supposed to know what was going on all around them, and one never mentioned doubtful subjects in the presence of gentlemen. Lord Melbourne when Prime Minister would not allow the young Queen Victoria to see the Acts containing the vice regulations, and even after her marriage nothing was done until after the Prince Consort's death. One cannot help thinking that Queen Victoria probably knew a great deal more than Melbourne realized. All her life she lived in fear that the less pleasant traits of her uncles would be repeated in her own children.

It was during the time the Butlers were in Oxford that Josephine became so deeply involved in the campaign which was officially

The exterior and interior of the Chapel of the Holy Trinity,
Old Bewick

Josephine Butler, nineteenth-century crusader,
portrait by G. F. Watts

designated 'The Ladies National Association For The Abolition Of Government Regulations of Vice'. In her own words she has described how she prayed for a very long time for guidance, until quite sure where her vocation lay. Once she had decided she never gave up until the battle was won. The battle was to last for many years; it was not until February 1886 that the Acts she so hated were finally repealed.

Josephine Butler was never a strong woman, and the Oxford air did not suit her constitution. After a few years the family moved to Cheltenham, where one of the great sorrows of her life took place. Her small daughter Evangeline, who was then 5 years old, was upstairs when she heard her father coming into the house. Dashing as children do she fell over the banisters to the ground floor, where she died almost immediately. A marble bust of poor little Evangeline has a place of honour in Miss Hetha Butler's home. It is typically Victorian, even to a dove perched on the child's arm. Josephine and George Butler became the parents of three sons, the eldest being the father of Miss Hetha Butler, whose home was at Ewart near Wooler until a few years ago.

From Cheltenham the Butler family moved to Liverpool and it was there that Josephine, supported by her husband, became so active in her unpopular campaign. She must have found the atmosphere of genteel Cheltenham suffocating with all its smugness and respectability.

In a great port like Liverpool vice and squalor were accepted as a way of life, a way which Josephine and her supporters were determined to change. It is not my intention to give in detail the laws which she was trying to rectify. She has herself written of these at length in *The Great Crusade*, and in *Josephine Butler. An Autobiographical Memoir*, edited by George W. and Lucy A. Johnson, the campaign is dealt with in detail.

Part of the introduction to this memoir is worth quoting, as according to her grand-daughter it is such an accurate summing up of her character. James Stuart, M.A., L.L.D., in his introduction says:

She was a great reader of the bible, and a humble supplicant before the throne of God. But, while her own beliefs were clear and definite, she had no narrowness in her views. She had to endure much, especially in the early days of the crusade—the averted glances

4

of former friends—the brutal attacks of ignorant opponents—but the inspiration of a right purpose enabled her to rise above all that—and now what is the sum of it all? . . . the world as a whole is better because she has lived, and the seed that she has sown can never die.

Yet for all her strong religious beliefs she was never pious or censorious, she always remembered that "there but for the Grace of God go I". When the Prime Minister of the day, Gladstone met her for the first time he said, "I was struck by the force of her mind, and I thought her perfectly and remarkably feminine."

In a biography by E. Moberly Bell published in 1962, her work is dealt with in great detail. The foreword in this book is by R. A. Butler, now Lord Butler of Saffron Walden and Master of Trinity College, Cambridge, who is related to George Butler's family.

In 1928, the centenary of Josephine Butler's birth, her *Life* by Mrs. Fawcett marked the occasion. Millicent Fawcett was an ardent worker for womens' suffrage and was created a Dame of the British Empire. The Millicent Fawcett library in London houses boxes of Josephine Butler's letters. Josephine herself would not have welcomed these tributes to her memory. She left written instructions to her sons that "It is my special request that you will never allow anyone to think of writing a memoir of me. . . ." This however was a request that could not be carried out. People who enter public life and achieve fame such as Josephine Butler did cease to belong to themselves. They become part of history, and it is the price that has to be paid. I think she would have understood, even if she did not like the publicity.

Some brief mention must be made of the injustices she was combating. In the late eighteenth and for most of the nineteenth century there were in most of the ports and in the garrison towns licensed brothels and houses of ill-fame for the sailors and "the brutal and licentious soldiery". Prostitution flourished, and Josephine Butler, being a realist, recognized that it would always exist. It was the way the laws were administered that she was fighting. Any woman or girl found or suspected of soliciting could be arrested and subjected to the most humiliating and degrading medical examinations, which often resulted in the women sinking even deeper into depravity. These women often died early of disease and the ghastly conditions under which they existed. These were very different women from their high-class sisters who were tucked away by Victorian 'gentlemen' in little houses in St. John's Wood. The oldest profession in the world had its social distinctions, just as much as any other in Victorian England. Josephine Butler urged—and the society named after her has continued the policy throughout the years—that "the law must apply equally to all citizens, men and women". This was quoted recently in *The Shield*, which is published by the Josephine Butler Society, formerly the Association for Moral and Social Hygiene.

How a frail woman like Josephine Butler accomplished so much is almost miraculous. Not only was she a good wife and mother, but an inveterate traveller who journeyed all over the country for her 'Great Crusade'. She was never militant; all her work was done by her sincerity and persuasiveness and the charm which she was unaware she possessed. Her first venture into public speaking was at Crewe, where she addressed a tough crowd of railwaymen. She spoke in her own county, at Berwick, Alnwick and Morpeth. In her own words, she gives a vivid description of her experience at Morpeth. The clergyman whom she had hoped would take the chair for her declined, as he had voted in favour of the Vice Acts. (Hardly in keeping with the cloth, one would think.) A working man in the audience was persuaded to deputise, but not before he had rushed home and changed into his Sunday best! Her prose becomes poetic as she goes on to say that after the meeting was over she had to wait half an hour on Morpeth platform for the train to Newcastle. It was a bright moonlight night she says, and frosty too, making the grass in the fields resemble silver. She speaks of the silence which was suddenly broken by the approach of the train from the north. To appreciate her prose it is imperative to read *The Great Crusade*.

Into her home in Liverpool she took 'unfortunate' women, helping them in every way possible. At the same time she was still agitating for more support, which eventually she received. Many of the Quakers were on her side, and Florence Nightingale and Harriet Martineau were her supporters. As time went on many doctors and clergymen rallied to her cause, and Parliament had to realize she was no crank, but a dedicated and able woman who refused to be beaten.

In 1871 Josephine Butler was called to give evidence before a

Royal Commission in The House of Lords, the only woman in that then strictly male preserve. She came through her ordeal bravely, but it was fifteen years before the 'Great Crusade' was accomplished, years in which she never faltered or spared her frail constitution. Not only did she campaign in England, but her travels took her to the Continent, and she became a familiar figure in Switzerland.

At times she did have some relaxation, taking holidays in Europe with her husband and family, who nobly supported her in her work. Her motto was "Nothing endures that is founded on injustice", and by this motto she lived. There was nothing frumpish about this pioneer of social injustice. She dressed in a most elegant manner, and her grand-daughter says she always used the most beautiful scent. Which all goes to show it is not necessary to be a battle-axe, or the typical 'do-gooder' to rectify social wrongs. To use a current expression, the wrong image of social welfare has been built up and has antagonized a great many people.

George Butler, who had been made a Canon of Winchester, lived for four years after he saw his wife's campaign at last successful. He died in London in 1890. After his death Josephine became a prolific writer, not only writing the life of her husband, but also a life of her father, *John Grey of Dilston*.

One of the high-lights of her colourful career was the founding in 1870 of what is now known as the Josephine Butler Society, the object of which is that it "fights for an equal standard of morality and sexual responsibility for men and women". The centenary was celebrated in March 1970 by a dinner in The House of Lords, at which the writer was a guest. In Liverpool, appropriately, is the Josephine Butler Memorial House, where social workers are trained. Formerly the Josephine Butler Society laboured under the clumsy title of 'The Association for Moral and Social Hygiene'. Enough to put anyone off!

Josephine Butler was a widow for sixteen years, and towards the end of her life she came home to Northumberland. For a time she lived with her son at Ewart and then moved to the house in Wooler where she died.

The house is in Queen's Road and is a semi-detached stone-built house named Fallowfield. Miss Hetha Butler remembers going to see 'Grannie' there, and how she always gave her little presents, such as Japanese paper fans. She had very little money as she had spent it all in helping other people and financing her 'Great Crusade'. A more lasting present she gave to her grand-daughter is a miniature Sheraton grandmother clock which Miss Butler treasures today. The present was accompanied by a charming letter which is still preserved. Another delightfully human letter I read was about some birds she was sending to her grand-children "in a little cage". She never lost her love for 'all creatures great and small'. When she was a child at Dilston, a favourite dog Pincher died, and Josephine was quite sure that he had a soul. When her governess remonstrated with her about such a belief her unanswerable reply was, "Why not?"

As an old lady she wore a lace cap with mauve ribbons, and she retained her fragile beauty to the last.

On a December day in 1906, when snow covered the Cheviots Josephine Butler died in the country where she was born. She was 78. Her grave is in Kirknewton churchyard, under the shadow of Yeavering Bell. Kirknewton is only a short way from Milfield where this remarkable woman was born. It is fitting that she should rest in good Northumbrian soil. On the house in Wooler where she died is a plaque presented by Wooler Women's Institute; it was unveiled by her grand-daughter.

In her centenary year a Commemoration Service was held in Westminster Abbey on 24th April 1928. The Order of Service was as follows:

The hymn was "O God our help in ages past".

The lesson was from St. John. 8:1–11.

The anthem was Henry Vaughan's "Peace", the first verse of which is:

> My soul there is a country
> Far beyond the stars,
> Where stands a winged sentry
> all skilful in the wars.

This was followed by "He who would valiant be 'gainst all disaster", and the service ended with Blake's "Jerusalem".

On Friday 28th April a commemoration meeting was held in Liverpool, when the chairman, the Vice Chancellor of Liverpool University, described Josephine Butler as "the most distinguished woman of the nineteenth century". Other speakers were Dame

Rachel Crowdy; Ellen Wilkinson, M.P., the fiery member of Parliament for Jarrow on Tyne; and the Reverend G. Studdart Kennedy, M.C., M.A.

A talk by Lady Astor, M.P. (the first woman member ever returned to Westminster) on Josephine Butler's Life was broadcast from 9.15 to 9.35 p.m.

It is interesting to read where the tickets for the Liverpool meeting could be obtained, as it proves how wide were Josephine's contacts, with no barriers of creed or denomination: the Catholic Women's League, the Free Church Centre, the Jewish Welfare Centre and the Moral Welfare Board, Church House, all appear in the list.

Such were the tributes paid to a great Northumbrian. May her memory live on as a courageous and compassionate woman, and in the words of a Cheviot shepherd's wife, made quite recently to Josephine's grand-daughter, "As a heroine."

4

The Doctor Syntax Story

'Bring forth the horse!'—the horse was brought;
In truth, he was a noble steed.

Byron. *Mazeppa*

Some readers may think it incongruous that a chapter describing the life and work of a great social reformer such as Josephine Butler should be followed by the story of a racehorse. In the writer's opinion it is not so. The nineteenth-century crusader dearly loved all animals, and I am sure would have been one of the first to agree that horses can be heroes and heroines. Horses have a scroll of honour like human beings, and as long as there is racing in the world some of the famous names will be remembered. Diamond Jubilee, St. Simon and Persimmon, Ben d'Or and Mumtaz Mahal, 'The Flying Filly', were giants on the flat, while Golden Miller and Arkle made history in the world of chasing. Many jockeys too have been national heroes, from the great Fred Archer to Steve Donoghue and Sir Gordon Richards and the countless amateur and professional riders who have risked life and limb at Aintree. The writer has always loved racing, and remembers vividly the first meeting she ever attended, which was a Haydon point-to-point many years ago. Her mind was made up then that one day she would see a 'National', and this ambition was realized in 1954 when she travelled to Liverpool to see Bryan Marshal bring Royal Tan home in front of Tudor Line, who jumped sideways at the last fence. The day was made more memorable as the writer's money was on Royal Tan!

Six years ago she went to the Kelso Meeting to see the Scottish horse Freddie, who later ran second in the greatest steeplechase in the world.

Though many attempts have been made by them, a Scottish horse has still to win the 'National'. Old McMoffat, Wynburgh and Freddie were some of the 'Scotsmen' who only succeeded in getting a place. An ambition of the writer's not yet realized is to see a Derby. Those who say it is better to watch racing on television cannot have the love of racing in their blood. It is the reality and the excitement of being on a race-course and hearing the announcement "They're under starter's orders" that thrills one as no television programme ever can. It can never compare with the real thing. Vicarious pleasures have never appealed to me, and I would rather be frozen with cold, as I have been on many occasions, than sit in front of the 'box'. In 1969 I saw the 'National' in colour for the first time, and although I had the luck to back the first and second horses, Highland Wedding and Steel Bridge, I was longing to be at Aintree. For many years now I have seen the Northumberland Plate run at Gosforth Park, although I have never been so lucky on the flat as with the jumping.

In case people assume that I squander my substance with the bookies, I must enlighten them now. Four shillings on the tote, or half a crown with the bookies is my limit, though I must admit that I once was reckless enough to risk a pound on a 'dead cert'. I remember going through agonies during the race and almost crying with relief when 'my' horse was first past the winning post!

A dream of mine which will never be fulfilled is to own the winner of the Northumberland Plate and lead in the victor at the Park.

Loving horses and racing as I do it has been most exciting to trace the career and history of a horse which was one of the most famous ever to be owned by a Northumbrian. This was Doctor Syntax, whose story I am attempting to tell in this chapter.

It must be made very clear that the curious name is notable in three different contexts; as a fictional character, as a racehorse, and as the name of a public house at Stocksfield in Northumberland. To tell the story in chronological order it must start with the creator of the mythical doctor.

In 1741 there was born one William Coombe, who, until his death in 1823, spent a great deal of his life in King's Bench debtor's prisons. His was an eventful and chequered career, yet he was to gain his place in the *Dictionary of National Biography* by his creation of Doctor Syntax. Coombe has been described as an adventurer, which is probably the best way to convey the character of this extraordinary man. Known as 'Count Coombe' during his long life-time of eighty-two years, he was a private soldier, a cook, a waiter, a law student (we are not told where) and a London bookseller's hack. In spite of his variety of jobs he found time to be a prolific writer. His first success came with a satire, *The Diaboliad*, published in 1776. He cannot have gained financially from this success or he squandered his rewards in riotous living, as from 1780 he spent most of his time as a guest of His Majesty. His work included political pamphlets and letterpress for illustrated books, but the works for which he is remembered are *The Three Tours of Doctor Syntax*, written in 1812–20 and 1821.

The tours were entitled "In Search of The Picturesque", "In Search of Consolation" and "In Search of a Wife". Beside me as I write is a copy of Coombe's "In Search of The Picturesque", published by T. Noble, 79 Fleet Street, London. It must be admitted it is a dreadfully dull little book, and most of the verse is written in the rhythmic beat of iambic pentameter. It is doubtful if "The Tours" would be remembered at all were it not for the fact that the illustrations are by Thomas Rowlandson. A typical example of Coombe's verse is the following on the frontispiece of "In Search of the Picturesque";

> The Doctor, finding danger near,
> Flew swiftly on the wings of fear,
> And nimbly clamber'd up a tree,
> That gave him full security.

This could never be classed as great verse.

Originally called "The Schoolmaster's Tour", "In Search of the Picturesque" was first published in *The Poetical Magazine* in 1813. After the title changed various editions were published until 1903, yet today Coombe is almost forgotten.

I admit that until I began to trail Doctor Syntax the horse, I had never heard of the creator of the literary doctor. Tracing a story is what I imagine a detective hunt must be like. One clue leads to another, and gradually the pattern is formed, rather like a jig-saw puzzle. Often there is a missing piece of the puzzle which eludes one, and until that can be traced the pattern is incomplete. Another danger is that so many people have a different version of the same story and it is sometimes nearly impossible to sift the fact from the fiction as each vouches for his veracity.

Even the best authorities are in conflict at times, I have just noticed that in another reference to Coombe he is described as a doctor; as there are no references to his ever having included medicine in his varied assortment of careers, one only assumes that some confusion has arisen in connection with his mythical character.

Thomas Rowlandson who illustrated *The Tours* was born in 1756. He settled in London where he made a name for himself as a portrait painter, until he forsook this for caricatures and illustrations. Among the writers whose books he illustrated were Smollett, Goldsmith and Sterne. Some short time ago when visiting a friend's house in the Longhorsley district of Northumberland, the writer's attention was drawn to a set of blue Staffordshire plates, and on examination discovered that the pictorial designs illustrated *The Tours of Doctor Syntax*.

If Coombe's creation has been almost obscured in the mists of time, that of the doctor's equine namesake has most certainly not. When the horse was christened the name must have been a household one, curious though it is. It is such a dull name, reminding one of school days, and, in the writer's case at least, the struggle to master the intricacies of English Grammar.

The equine Doctor was foaled at Hunmanby in East Yorkshire in 1811. His owner being Squire Humphrey Osbaldestone. In those days racehorses took their ages from 1st May not from 1st January, as they do now. This is all most confusing for the layman, and is best explained by using an 'Irishism' that in fact a 2-year-old has not often reached that age when first raced. The sire of Doctor Syntax was Paynator, and his dam was an unnamed mare by Beningbrough. His ancestry on the maternal side can be traced to about 1685, therefore Syntax, like many racehorses has his name in the Horse *Debrett* and can rank as an old county family! The Doctor was sold as a 2-year-old to a Mr. Knapton for 125 guineas on the 12th July 1813, two years before Waterloo. The future champion's first race was at Catterick, where meetings are still held today. In his first race Doctor Syntax fell; the only other occasion that this horse ever came down was in his last race. The second owner of Doctor Syntax, Mr. Knapton, was landlord of 'The Star Inn', Stonegate, York, and kept a small stud at

Huntington, not far from the city of York. In 1814 the Northumbrian story of Doctor Syntax began. He was bought by Mr. Ralph Riddell of Felton. The Riddell family has a pedigree even longer than that of the horse which was to bring them so many racing trophies.

As far back as the year 1500 a Thomas Riddell was Sheriff of the City of Newcastle, and three times between 1510 and 1527 he was mayor. This record of public service was maintained by Thomas Riddell's descendants. In 1601 to 1602 another Thomas Riddell was Sheriff of Newcastle and in the following year when James I passed through the city on his way from Edinburgh to London he conferred a knighthood on Thomas Riddell. It is said that King James was so overwhelmed by the reception that he received on Tyneside that he exclaimed "By ma saul, they are enough to spoil a good king."

Later in the seventeenth century Thomas Riddell, having acquired property in Gateshead on the south side of the Tyne, left Northumberland and lived for many years at what was then known as Gateshead House.

Descendants of Sir Thomas returned to their native county and founded the Swinburne Castle, Felton and Cheeseburn Grange branches of the family. The Riddells are one of the Northumbrian families who have remained faithful to the old religion of Roman Catholicism, consequently there has been a great deal of inter-marriage and it is extremely difficult to disentangle the relationships. Twice there have been marriages between Riddells and Widdringtons, when heiresses have brought more property into the family. In 1726 Thomas Riddell married Mary Widdrington, co-heiress to the Cheeseburn estate. To complicate matters even more, the son of this Thomas married another Widdrington (I have been told they were cousins), and this heiress, Elizabeth, brought the Felton Park estate into the family. A picture of Elizabeth Riddell (Widdrington) by Sir Joshua Reynolds was bought by the Committee of the Laing Art Gallery in Newcastle. This Elizabeth was the grandmother of Ralph Riddell, the owner of Doctor Syntax. Cheeseburn Grange is about 12 miles equidistant from Newcastle, Hexham and Morpeth. It has a most attractive setting in well-wooded parkland. The house is of the Gothic type of architecture and was partly rebuilt by Dobson the great Newcastle architect of the early nineteenth century.

In the autumn of last year, when driving along the road past Cheeseburn Grange, the writer saw the Tynedale hunt drawing a covert. The road winds its way to a cross-roads where a sign-post points the way to Stamfordham on the left and Ponteland on the right. Sitting beside the signpost, as though wondering which road to take, was a fox! Before there was time to seize a camera Reynard was off, outwitting the hounds who were cubbing. It is a sight I never expect to see again.

Felton Park, another Riddell estate, lies north of Morpeth off the great North Road, and close to the village of the same name. Swinburne Castle in north Tyndale is no longer occupied.

This was the kind of family which Doctor Syntax joined, to add lustre to their name in the world of racing. He would feel quite at home in such surroundings; and in his years of glory when he waited for the cheers of the crowds as he passed the winning post he would prick his ears with delight, as another famous horse Brown Jack did in this century. Doctor Syntax outrivalled Brown Jack's record of successes, a fact which is sometimes overlooked.

Ralph Riddell, who bought Doctor Syntax, had become the owner of Felton Park in 1798, and was already a successful owner when the Doctor joined his stable. X.Y.Z. was one of the most famous of the string. A verse in his praise is quoted here:

> The bets flew round frae side to side;
> 'The field agyen XY' they cried:
> We'd hardly time to lay 'em a'
> When in he cam, Hurraw! Hurraw!
> 'Gad smash!' say aw, 'XY's the steed,
> He bangs them a' for pith an' speed,
> We never see'd the like, man!'

Another of Mr. Riddell's horses on the scroll of fame was Don Carlos, which was ultimately bought by the Russian Government and exported to that country. Famous though these two horses were, they never attained the glory nor the admiration that Doctor Syntax did. A grandson of the Doctor's, Newminster out of Beeswing, sired the Derby winner of 1867, The Hermit. This Derby winner bought by Henry Chaplin for a thousand guineas was the cause of great rivalry between his owner and the notorious Marquis of Hastings.

Doctor Syntax was a small brown horse, only standing 15 hands high, but he had the heart of a lion. He was trained partly at his owner's home at Felton and partly at Middleham in Yorkshire, which is still a famous training centre.

It would be tedious to enumerate all the Doctor's successes. Apart from his two falls, and the odd occasion when he was only placed, his was a success story rarely equalled in the annals of Turf history.

It is sad that many of the meetings where he ran are no longer in the calendar. When three years of age he won five races at Preston, Morpeth and Richmond. Preston race-course closed down in 1848, while Morpeth's racing days ended in 1883. It is not known when racing began at Morpeth, but it was well established by 1720.

In 1775 *The Newcastle Journal* announced that "The Stewards of Morpeth Races, desirous that all ranks of people might partake of the general satisfaction, so apparent at the meeting, humanely ordered five pounds of the subscription money to be distributed amongst the prisoners in the jail, an example worthy of imitation." Later the same newspaper reports that "The nimble fingered gentry were busy at Morpeth races last week." One wonders if some of these gentry ended up in Morpeth gaol! By 1800 Newcastle and Morpeth were the only two meetings in the calendar in Northumberland. In September a plate given by the Earl of Carlisle was won by Mr. Riddell's Walnut.

In the Sporting Magazine of 1831 is the following report:

Morpeth are the only minor races in Northumberland which have continued to exist in spite of the falling-off of the patrons and promoters of the Turf in that county. Alnwick has long since ceased to exist as a place of sport; Hexham can only boast of the contests of ponies and jackasses, whilst the nature of the course at Tynemouth, formed on the sands, presents an insuperable obstacle to the introduction of superior cattle. Although Morpeth possesses the advantage of a piece of turf, to the improvement of which great attention is paid, although it is in the midst of a rich and populous neighbourhood, symptoms of decline have for many years been showing themselves, as well in the sport as in the company. More decidedly in the former, but even the latter is far, far from what it was in my youthful days. A tolerable ordinary lunch is mustered the first day, aided by the never failing haunch of venison from Mr. Riddell of Felton Park, and contributions of game and

fruit from various quarters. After dinner, subscriptions are col-
lected towards the plate for the following year and an attempt made
at a Hunter's stake. The dinner on the second day generally resembles
rather a private party than a public table. The dinner hour is two
o'clock, and the start for the course at three, or as soon after as may
be. There is a ball on the first evening and theatrical amusements at
both.

The writer goes on to describe the Morpeth course which was
at Cottingwood. He is nostalgic for the old days and deplores
that even Mr. Riddell "who has supported them staunchly till
now had not a horse there".

I have quoted so much from this unknown writer's saga of
regrets because it is so typical that "things are never what they
used to be". Every generation repeats the same lamentations, never
pausing to think that it is they who have changed as well as
other people and places. The past is so often seen through rose-
coloured spectacles, and there is no one left to contradict the
tales of things as they "used to be". No one regrets the passing
of old traditions and customs more than I do, especially when
changes are made simply for the sake of change. Yet one must be
realistic and admit that in some cases changes have been made for
the better, and nowhere more so than in the world of racing.
Although horses are still nobbled and 'got at', the penalties are
severe, and any jockey, however famous, is cautioned for dis-
obeying rules. Nowhere has that been proved more fully than in
the case of a leading jockey like Lester Piggot. Horses are not
over-raced so much as they used to be, and veterinary Surgeons
and first-aid members are obligatory at all meetings. It is horrible
when a horse is injured and has to be destroyed; but on the other
hand, I know if I were a horse and had the choice I would rather
be destroyed on a racecourse than end in a knacker's yard.

There are many worse forms of entertainment than the sport of
kings, and, in this day, the sport of queens. For reasons known
only to herself, Queen Victoria did not approve of racing;
perhaps that made her son and heir all the keener on the sport
which he did so much to popularize. No one who was there, or
saw on television the collapse of Devon Loch in the 'National' of
1956, will ever forget the surge of sympathy for the Queen Mother.
It is reputed when commiserating with Dick Francis, Devon
Loch's jockey, Her Majesty said, "That's racing, I suppose."

Mr. Ralph Riddell had more than his share of luck during the years when his colours were carried to victory at so many northern meetings. As an owner he changed his colours three times. At first they were a black and yellow stripe, then in 1814 they became a blue and yellow stripe and pink cap, and finally in 1828 blue and yellow quartered. From the age of 3 until he was 12 Doctor Syntax carried these changing colours to victory on thirty-six occasions at Preston, Morpeth, Richmond and Catterick, at Middleham and Lancaster. He ran forty-nine races and only failed to pass the winning post thirteen times. In J. Fairfax-Blakeborough's *Northern Turf History* he relates how once he was the guest of Mr. Cuthbert Riddell at Swinburne Castle the table was decorated with gold cups won by Doctor Syntax. I have tried without success to trace the names of the jockeys who rode the famous horse. The trainer who handled him at Middleham was John Lonsdale, but his jockeys strangely enough are anonymous.

A verse from a poem by Will. H. Ogilvie is appropriate to these forgotten men.

> Then his hands will reach for a fancied rein,
> And his shoulders forward slip,
> As he calls on a good game horse again,
> And brings him under the whip.
>
> And long may the lonely horseman ride
> In the firelight's rosy gleam,
> Ere the shadows from either side,
> And darkness, end his dream.
>
> From "The Old Horseman's Dream".

Doctor Syntax brought fame and fortune to his Northumbrian owner; and, though the horse was Yorkshire bred, he spent most of his life in his adopted county of Northumberland. He was 27 years of age when he was destroyed in 1838.

In Northumberland Doctor Syntax is commemorated in the name of a public house at New Ridley, which is a hamlet a little south of Stocksfield in Tynedale. The inn sign displays a picture of the famous 'Doctor'. There is another inn of the same name not far away at Prudhoe, but it has no historical significance. The only other known inn to bear the name is at Oldham in Lancashire; and as the horse raced so much in the duchy, presumably it is named after him. A record of this great horse's victories hangs in the inn at New Ridley.

For some time I was puzzled and curious to know what connection the four-legged Doctor Syntax had with New Ridley. It seemed a far cry from Felton on the Coquet. A visit to the inn solved the puzzle. When the horse was taken by road from Felton to race west of the Pennines a halt was made at New Ridley. A glance at the ordnance map will show that this would be just about the distance a horse would travel in one day. It was not until 1836 that Lord George Bentinck had the revolutionary idea of a 'horse-box' on wheels. He successfully transported his horse Ellis to Doncaster and won the St. Leger. There were no such luxuries for Mr. Riddell's horse, he hacked to all his meetings.

The village of New Ridley belies its name, as its history goes back for at least 500 years; and before it became an inn 'The Doctor Syntax' is thought to have been a blacksmith's shop.

The present inn stands in a row of stone-built cottages looking west over the Stocksfield burn and the green undulating grassland that rolls onwards towards the busy highway to Scotland: Dere Street or, more prosaically, the A.68. This is delightfully unspoilt country which west of Dere Street merges into Slaley Forest and that part of Northumberland which is Hexhamshire. The inn has been modernized by the owners, who are Scottish and Newcastle Breweries, but, in spite of the alterations, 'The Doctor Syntax' maintains its character of a country pub. Some of Thomas Rowlandson's illustrations of the fictional Doctor hang in the lounge.

A hundred years ago and long after the horse had gone to the green pastures the inn was famous in quite another way.

The house was inhabited by a family whose name was Stobbart and who made medicines and ointments from herbs in the bar parlour. Their green salve and pink ointment became famous and were sold in the city of Newcastle. Green salve cured boils, burns and sprains, while pink ointment had no limitations; it could be used for anything! The Stobbarts walked miles in search of herbs which they ground by hand; it is said they went as far afield as Shotley on the Durham border in their search for medicinal herbs. Mr. Stobbart was also a bone setter, and even performed minor operations—a most versatile gentleman. When this self-appointed medicine man died, his wife remained as proprietor

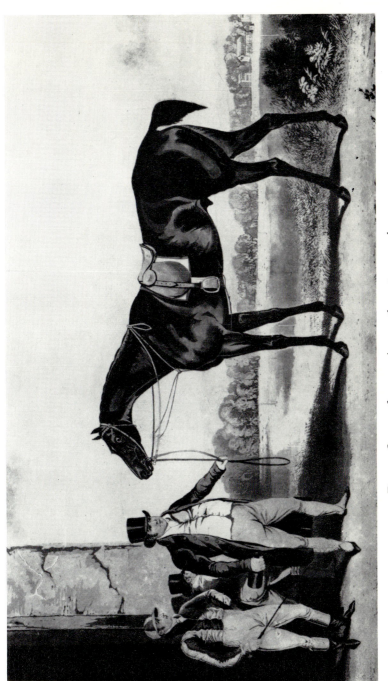

Doctor Syntax, famous nineteenth-century racehorse

Nunnykirk, home of the Orde family, and the ground where
Beeswing galloped long ago

of the inn and kept up a supply of patent medicines for the Newcastle shops and public houses. It therefore seems doubly appropriate that the inn should bear the name of Doctor.

British blood-stock owes much to this small brown horse. One of his offspring whose story is told later in this book became as famous as her sire, the gallant mare Beeswing.

The 'Doctor' won twenty-four gold cups, which when they were sold brought more than 500 guineas. Scattered now are the trophies of victory, but the memory of the horse lives on; he had such a curious name for a racehorse that curiosity makes people ask more about him than perhaps they would if he had been given a more ordinary name.

Some lines from "Good Hunting" by Dulce Morland apply not only to hunters but to gallant racehorses too, and Doctor Syntax was one of the most gallant.

> There's a great grass country in heaven,
> Where all good sportsmen go,
> And hounds and hunters who loved the chase,
> While they sojourned here below;
> And all the horses who did their best
> Still carry their masters there,
> While the old and tired and lame ones rest
> In clover beyond compare.

5

NUNNYKIRK AND BONNY BEESWING:
A House and a Horse

Come all ye jolly sportsmen of high and low degree,
And if you please attention pay a moment unto me;
While I of Bonny Beeswing sing, a galloper renown'd,
For she hath won her weight in gold and is with glory crown'd.

Anon

Nunnykirk, one of Northumberland's many 'big' houses is about
9 miles north-west of Morpeth, and stands in parkland watered by
the River Font, which is a tributary of the Wansbeck. Here in
1833 was foaled the famous racehorse Beeswing. The mare was
sired by the equally famous Doctor Syntax, out of a mare given to
Mr. William Orde of Nunnykirk by Mr. Ralph Riddell of Felton,
the owner of the 'Doctor'. Although her sire brought fame and
glory to his owner and broke many turf records, he was never
loved to the extent his daughter was. She became the pitman's idol
and was known throughout her racing career as 'The Pride of The
North'. Beeswing, unlike her sire, was Northumbrian born and
bred, he was an 'incomer' to Northumberland, although his
years of glory were those when he was Northumbrian owned and
domiciled. Legend has it that the pitmen loved the mare so much,
and she had won them so much money, that they carried her
shoulder-high off the course at Newcastle after one of her many
victories on her home ground. One link Doctor Syntax and
Beeswing have in common is that both were owned by members
of old Northumbrian families, and it is impossible to separate the
history of the horses from that of the owners. The Ordes of
Nunnykirk are one of the many county families who have given
stalwart service to Northumberland for generations. The name is
mentioned as long ago as 1362, when Simon de Orde died at the
village of East Ord on Tweedside. The family also owned

lands at Norham, which is not far from East Ord. Like so many Northumbrian families the Ordes stayed within the boundaries of their county, although they did forsake their Border home to venture as far south as the market town of Morpeth! Orde House in Morpeth was only demolished recently to make way for a garage. One of the family, William, was High Sheriff in the reign of Charles I, and the present holder of this ancient office is Mr. David Orde of Nunnykirk. A study of the list of High Sheriffs of Northumberland reveals how many of the same families have carried on what might be called a tradition of public service. One Orde was member of Parliament for Berwick in 1713, and many have been magistrates both in Northumberland and the neighbouring county of Durham, where at one time they owned land. Nunnykirk came into the possession of the family by the marriage of Ordes and Wards (this sounds like a horrible pun.) Twice did an Orde marry a Ward, to make matters even more complicated. I cannot decide which is the more difficult—to trace the pedigree of a family or that of a horse; both have their pitfalls, and it is so easy to make a slip.

Nunnykirk, as its name implies, was originally ecclesiastical property. It was granted by a De Merley of Morpeth to the Abbot of Newminster Abbey, who built a chapel and a tower, no traces of which remain. Newminster occurs in the name of Beeswing's son, who sired a Derby winner. The Church and the Turf are both commemorated in this famous name! It is thought that Nunnykirk at one time in its history was a house of rest for pilgrims on their way from Newminster to Hexham Priory. Newminster Abbey, of which only fragmentary remains can be seen, stands on the south bank of the river Wansbeck, close to the town of Morpeth. It was originally a Cistercian foundation and was a place of some importance in medieval times. Ranulph de Merley and his wife were buried there, and the notorious baron Umfraville, 'Robin Mend-the-Market', found a last resting place there. Ironically the name Newminster has more significance to those who study the Stud Book, than to students of medieval history. After Nunnykirk ceased to be ecclesiastical property it was owned by the Greys of Chillingham, until it passed into the ownership of the Wards and subsequently by marriage to the Orde family.

The breeder and owner of Beeswing for all her racing career was

William Orde. He had never expected to inherit the estate, but the early death of his elder brother made him heir to Nunnykirk. This second son had read for the Bar and was practising in London when in 1814 his father died and he succeeded to the Northumbrian property. He immediately gave up his practice at the Bar and came home to Northumberland to live the life of a country gentleman of those days. He employed the Newcastle architect, John Dobson, to carry out additions and improvements to the old house, which were completed in 1825. Nunnykirk has been described as the finest of Dobson's earlier houses. The house is domed, and inside is a central oblong hall and gallery from which the rooms radiate. The ceiling is exceptionally fine and has recently been redecorated. The Ionic columns of the main garden side give the house the Greek appearance of which Dobson was a master. It was in these delightful surroundings that Beeswing was born. Already Mr. Orde was the owner of Tomboy, who was the winner of the first Northumberland Plate, then run on the Town Moor at Newcastle. Tomboy also won the Gold Cup at Durham in 1832, the Gold Cups at Pontefract and Newcastle, a Silver Tureen at Stockton and more Gold Cups at Richmond, Doncaster and Newcastle in 1834.

Triumphant though Tomboy was, he was to be eclipsed by the gallant Beeswing. Her name will never be forgotten in her native Northumberland nor in the annals of racing. Her record was such that she outnumbered the victories of those eighteenth-century giants of racing, Flying Childers and Eclipse. Mr. David Orde of Nunnykirk has supplied me with the following information:

Beeswing was bred by William Orde of Nunnykirk, Northumberland, and was owned by him throughout her racing career. William Orde, who was unmarried, died in 1843 and was succeeded as squire of Nunnykirk by his nephew, Charles William Orde. Beeswing became his property and was owned by him throughout her stud career. Beeswing ran 64 times, winning 51 races (in 9 of which she walked over) and being placed second nine times, third once, fourth once and unplaced twice. She was trained by Robert Johnson and ridden by him in some of her early races, but he refused to ride again when the judge would not place her in the Doncaster St. Leger, though those who were present were convinced that she was second. She was ridden by Cartwright after this. Robert Johnson continued to take charge of her when she retired to the stud.

Stud Record

1844	chestnut colt	Old Port	By Sir Hercules
1845	barren		To Lanercost
1846	black colt	Nunnykirk	By Touchstone
1847	bay filly	Bonny Bee	By Galanthus
1848	bay colt	Newminster	By Touchstone.
1849	brown colt	Norham	By Birdcatcher
1850	black filly	Honey-dew	By Touchstone
1851	brown filly	Honey-suckle	By Touchstone
1852	black filly	(dead)	By Touchstone
1853	barren		To The Flying Dutchman
1854	died in March carrying a foal by The Flying Dutchman.		

Mr. Orde goes on to say that Nunnykirk was exported to France, where he was a sire for a short time. Newminster, about whom we have already heard, was the leading sire in 1859 and 1863, and his descendants were also leading sires in their day. Honey-dew and Honey-suckle, the daughters of Touchstone, bred several winners, and their descendants carried on the great tradition of the blood. Old Port raced only a few times, and does not appear to have been sent to stud. Bonny Bee was never on a race-course, but she was the dam and ancestress of winners. Poor Norham (named no doubt after the Orde property on Tweedside) died before his racing career began.

Touchstone, by whom Beeswing had five foals, of which one was born dead, was also one of the great horses of the nineteenth century. Owned by the Marquis of Westminster, Touchstone was a rank outsider for the St. Leger of 1834, and astonished even his owner and jockey when he won this classic in the Racing Calendar at odds of forty to one! He followed up this victory with many successes before he went to stud. It is interesting to read what the stud fees of a Classic winner were in those days. In 1838, when he served forty mares, the fee was thirty guineas, which was increased after three years to forty. He won over £30,000 for the Marquis of Westminster, who, so the story goes, when asked by some Americans to name his price for the horse, replied: "The American Dominions and nothing less." At the St. Leger meeting of 1835 Beeswing carried off the Champagne Stakes, and among those who saw the gallant mare from Northumberland gallop to victory were the Duchess of Kent and Princess Victoria. The Flying Dutchman, who sired Beeswing's last foal, which caused the mare's death at the age of 21, was also one of the great horses of history. It was at the York meeting of 1851 that a match between The Flying Dutchman and Voltigeur was run to decide which was the greatest of these two, both of them Derby and St. Leger winners. The race was run on the Knavesmire and attracted huge crowds, who saw The Flying Dutchman beat his rival. As was usual in those days the event was described in verse, some of which is as follows;

> To The Flying Dutchman drink success, who has so nobly run,
> He beat the famous Voltigeur and showed them how t'was done.
> Upon the thirtieth day of May in 1851,
> The Flying Dutchman and Voltigeur upon York course did run;
> 'Twas for a thousand sovereigns, believe me what I say,
> Which The Flying Dutchman has won and borne the prize away.

The Ordes made sure that their mare was only mated with the best blood.

As in the case of Beeswing's sire, Doctor Syntax, it would be tedious to enumerate all the races in which 'The Pride of the North' ran, the story is so graphically told in verse which I am including in full and is as follows:

Bonny Beeswing

> So drink a health to Beeswing for the deeds that she has done,
> At Newcastle, York, and Doncaster, many prizes she has won.
> Her Pedigree I will make known, if you the same require,
> And tell you what they call'd her dam, and what her noble sire;
> With all the cups that she has won, and purses fill'd with gold,
> Since in the racing calendar her name has been enroll'd.

> The Champagne Stakes at Doncaster, she won when two years old;
> Beside a thousand pounds or more of Sovereigns made of gold;
> And at Newcastle on the Tyne, I solemnly declare,
> A silver waggon was the prize of this distinguished mare.

> And near unto Newcastle town was bonny Beeswing bred,
> Where by her master 'Squire Orde, she frequently was fed;
> And now she has won many golden cups which on his table shine,
> When he with lords and ladies fair is known to take his wine.

> At Richmond and Northallerton believe me when I say,
> That she at both these races hath bore a prize away;
> At Lincoln she walk'd over, for neither friends nor foes,
> Would try with bonny Beeswing for fear that they should lose.

Now Beeswing is a gallant mare of courage stout and bold,
Her colour is a bright bay, and she is nine years old;
Her rider dressed in blue and white so gallant does appear,
At Doncaster races too the cup she won last year.

At Stockton and at Chester too, at Kelso and elsewhere,
The sporting world has been surpris'd at this North flying mare;
How speed and bottom all confess, surpass'd can be by none,
The truth of what my song declares, is prov'd by what she's done.

At Newcastle Charles XII, this year did see her tail.
As many empty purses show, and betting books explain;
The knowing coves from out the south must now to Beeswing bow,
As drooping heads and pockets light for them too plainly show.

Her dam was Cleopatra, The Doctor was her sire,
From them she got her mettle and from them she got her fire;
Twenty-one gold cups she won my boys, besides such lots of gold,
As never yet was won before, not can I here unfold.

At Ascot by the Queen's command, this noble mare did run,
A splendid cup of gold the prize, so gallantly she won;
May fortune smile upon her then, and on her steps attend,
So now my jolly sportsmen my song is at an end.

It would be interesting to know who composed this record of
Bonny Beeswing. It has obviously appeared in a local newspaper,
but the only information is that it was printed by P. Blair of
Morpeth towards the end of the mare's racing career. The
unknown poet, who scorned the laws of metre and scansion, also
indulged in poetic licence and exaggerated some of Beeswing's
achievements, which needed no embroidering. On 21st June
1841 at Newcastle races, Charles XII beat Beeswing by a short
head, so the poet took more licence when he says "At Newcastle,
Charles XII this year did see her tail", could he not be content that
the gallant little mare won the Gold Cup at the same meeting. He
is quite correct when he says,
"And at Newcastle on the Tyne I solemnly declare,
A silver waggon was the prize of this distinguished mare."
At Nunnykirk today is the silver waggon, which is composed of
350 separate pieces of silver and bears the following inscription:
"Newcastle Races. 1837. Won by Beeswing 25 June 1838.
Success to the coal trade. Presented by George Baker Esqr; of
Elemore Hall when in the 84th year of his age.

The waggon bears the Newcastle coat of arms, and is as attractive as it is unique. It is used as a fruit bowl. Legend has it that the waggon was subscribed for by the pitmen of the Northumberland coalfield as a mark of their appreciation of Beeswing, and this legend has sometimes been accepted as fact. The truth is that it was Mr. George Baker, of Elemore Hall, County Durham, who gave the trophy as a contribution to the local races in 1837 "in acknowledgement of the many acts of kindness he had received from the inhabitants of Newcastle".

At the June meeting at Newcastle, a race is named the Beeswing Handicap, "a plate of 700 Sovereigns for three year olds and upwards". Beeswing's memory is still green in Northumberland. When Mr. Orde's famous mare came home after a victory the bells of St. Nicholas' were ringing to welcome the pitman's idol.

When Beeswing's racing career came to an end in 1842, shortly before the death of her owner, the mare was the toast of Tyneside and the county of Northumberland. Public houses were named after her (only one remains, and that is in Felling, County Durham), and steamboats and coaches bore her name. Even hats, pipes and sweets were named after this heroine of the horse world. China mugs bore the magic name, and I understand there are still some in existence, although I have not been fortunate enough to see one myself. An antique shop in Morpeth's Newgate Street is 'The Beeswing', and a picture of the mare can be seen there. There is a story that when this house was a tavern, Beeswing used to be stabled there when she was on her way to Nunnykirk. Like her father Doctor Syntax, she would travel by road, and it is quite probable that the journey was broken in Morpeth. So many legends have gathered round this most famous of all Northumbrian horses that with the passing of time it is almost impossible to vouch for the authenticity of many of them.

At the end of the racing season of 1842 Beeswing retired, and in the autumn of that year Mr. William Orde died, at the age of 68. The *Historical Register* records that

Died, at Morpeth, William Orde, Esq; of Nunnykirk, Northumberland, universally, and deservedly respected. The deceased, who was widely known as the owner of the celebrated Beeswing, Tomboy and other racers, as well as by some little eccentricities of dress and deportment, was honoured, not only in Great Britain, but on the

Continent, for a character which few have acquired—an honest and honourable sportsman. He was at the great fête at Ravensworth, and promenaded a considerable time on the lawn. He appeared in good spirits and, conversed freely all round.

How fascinating it would be to know what Mr. Orde's eccentricities of dress and deportment were! Mr. Orde was asked once what price he would take for his Bonny Beeswing and he replied that she could not be sold, she belonged to the people of Northumberland. This sentiment expresses exactly what the local pride in Beeswing was, she "belonged to Northumberland".

Mr. William Orde never married, and he was succeeded at Nunnykirk by his nephew Mr. Charles Orde, who owned his uncle's famous mare throughout her stud career. This Squire of Nunnykirk was for many years Chairman of Quarter Sessions for the County of Northumberland. Mr. Orde made news in those days by a speech he made at a dinner of the Northumberland Show Society (now the County Show, which is held at Alnwick). Those were the days of bonnets and crinolines, and when Mr. Orde rose to propose the toast of "The Ladies" he said, "May their virtues be as large as their crinolines, and their faults as small as their bonnets." These remarks would be considered highly daring in the Victorian era. Mr Charles Orde died in 1875 at Nunnykirk.

For the next twelve years of Beeswing's life she was almost continually in foal. Out of her eleven matings she was only twice barren, which gave the over-worked mother a breathing space. Only one of her foals was stillborn, and five of her offspring survived her. It seems so tragic that this gallant little mare died in foal. Her life must have been a hard one. Even the more considerate owners over-raced their horses in those days, and out of her twenty-one years of life, seven were spent racing and the rest bringing more winners into the world. The blood of Beeswing can be traced in many horse's pedigrees today. She certainly earned her keep. It was on 4th March 1854 that Beeswing died, without doubt the most loved, and the most lovable racehorse Northumberland has ever produced.

After her death the legends began to multiply, and are told, usually inaccurately, to this day. One which persists in the Stewartry of Kirkcudbrightshire is that the owner of 'The Pride of the North' bought an inn half way between Dumfries and

Dalbeattie and called it Beeswing. To any Northumbrian this is so absurd as to be discounted at once. No Orde of Nunnykirk was ever an inn-keeper. Yet there are those unacquainted with the history of Northumberland who believe this ridiculous story. On 23rd August 1961, the following piece of misinformation appeared under the heading of "Your Village" in a local newspaper *The Standard*: "Beeswing was originally a horse. It was a race-horse, and was successful. Tradition says that it won the Derby. Anyhow its owner built or bought an inn, and called it Beeswing."

This distortion of fact is enough to make Beeswing and her owners turn in their graves. In 1852 a Nathaniel Caven was landlord of 'The Beeswing Inn', this entry appears in the Commercial Directory of Scotland. Some enterprising landlord may have cashed in on the popularity and fame of Northumberland's idol, and named his inn after her; or it could be that a groom or stable lad who once looked after Beeswing made his way over the Border and thus commemorated her name. It is impossible to solve this mystery now. I have made every effort without any success. The County Library in Dumfries accepts the tale that was circulated in *The Standard*, and I quote from a letter. "It appears that the owner of Beeswing bought an inn which he named after the horse, and that the village later took the name of the inn. I hope this information is of some use to you." Whatever evidence is produced now, this legend appears to have become accepted north of the Border, and I doubt whether it will ever be clarified. To paraphrase a line of Scotland's Rabbie Burns, "O'wad the power the giftie gie us, to hear ourselves as others hear us, It wad frae many a blunder free us and foolish notion." I can only hope that my research has vindicated the memory of the Ordes and Beeswing. Though they might not have rejected the rumour that the Derby was numbered among her victories.

As I, myself am so interested in horses and racing I had heard of Beeswing for as long as I can remember, but until I decided to trace her astonishing career I really knew very little about her and her life. I was delighted when I received a letter from a member of the Orde family now living in the South of England who said, "Please in your next book do include the Ordes of Nunnykirk and also the famous mare Beeswing. There are still a lot of her trophies at Nunnykirk." This request settled the matter, and I have enjoyed every moment of my search for information. I have come to love this wonderful mare, and as I am writing this I have beside me a reproduction of a painting of Beeswing and her first foal Old Port with Nunnykirk in the background. Beeswing has such an intelligent expression and is standing guard over the foal. That I have this picture and am able to reproduce it in this book is due to the kindness of Sir Charles Orde of Nunnykirk. Sir Charles and his family have given me much detailed information about the mare, and helped in every way possible. Last summer I spent a delightful day at Nunnykirk, where I lived and breathed Beeswing. I was shown many of the trophies won by her, including the famous silver waggon, and, most touching of all, her mounted hoofs. They seemed so small and delicate to have galloped so many miles. A 'ride' from the grounds to the fields beyond the Font is called Beeswing's gallop to this day, and at the far end is her 'hemmel' a truly Northumbrian word to be found in Heslop's *Dictionary of Northumberland Words*. For those who are not familiar with Northumbrianisms a 'hemmel' is a shed open on all four sides, in which an animal can shelter. At Nunnykirk is the picture of Beeswing by Herring senior painted in 1842, the year when she retired from the turf. Now, more than a hundred years after Beeswing's death, her magic has not dimmed. The prosaic entry in local records reporting her death has no place at Nunnykirk, where she is as much a part of the family as the owners themselves.

The pastures where Beeswing grazed at Nunnykirk were green on the July day of my visit and the little Font between its banks covered with flowers went on its way to meet the Wansbeck. Further up the stream from Nunnykirk is the Font Reservoir, which was dammed in the last century to provide water for the people of Tynemouth far away on the Northumbrian coast.

Plantations on the Nunnykirk estate are named after Beeswing and other famous horses owned by the Ordes; in fact wherever one goes there is some reminder of 'The Pride of the North'. It is always a sad feeling when a chapter closes, and I am loath to come to the end of the history of this dearly loved horse. I am reminded of Josephine Butler's question to her governess— "Have animals souls?"—and when she was told not to ask such a question, her reply was "Why not?" I feel inclined to make the same reply as Josephine. If there are green pastures for horses then Beeswing is surely there. She deserved all the praise and adulation she received in life, and now that her name is a memory she still deserves unqualified admiration. Men and women have written their names on the pages of Northumbrian history, and so has Beeswing. In Northumberland's scroll of fame her name should be emblazoned; she brought glory to her native county and has handed down to posterity her gallant spirit and indomitable courage. Nunnykirk and the land round it was a perfect setting for Bonny Beeswing. It is gentle grass country, serene and peaceful, and the epitome of the Orde's most famous horse.

I am so glad I have had this opportunity to see where my heroine lived; she seemed much nearer to me there than on a race-course. Perhaps she was glad when the winning post had been passed and she was on her way home to her 'hemmel' and her gallop. Unlike the anonymous composer of the Beeswing ballad, I have written, not sung the history of a house and a horse. To sing anyone's praises is such a trite expression and yet I cannot think of a more suitable way of describing this chapter, than to call it "In praise of Beeswing".

> They called her The Pride of the North,
> Squire Orde's game mare, Beeswing,
> To the praise of Northumberland's best loved horse,
> Let every sportsman sing.
>
> Anon.

6

Fallodon and a Foreign Secretary

'The lamps are going out all over Europe;
we shall not see them lit again in our lifetime.'

3rd August 1914. *Twenty-Five Years.*
Edward, Viscount Grey of Fallodon

Edward Grey, better known to posterity as Grey of Fallodon, is one of the outstanding figures in the political history of this country. The nineteenth and the early part of the present century were notable for the many great men who were statesmen and not politicians. These were the days of the two great parties, the Liberals and the Conservatives, and both sides produced men who in their different ways left their mark on the history of their country. None contributed more by his integrity and selfless devotion to duty than Edward Grey, who was Foreign Secretary when the First World War broke out. His words when he realized that war was inevitable are quoted at the beginning of this chapter and are immortalized in the history of the times.

Not only is Grey remembered as a statesman, but as one of the most greatly loved Northumbrians. He is one of those rare people as greatly loved in death as in life. He is an outstanding example to future generations of one who overcame the bitter blows fate dealt him in his personal life. His first wife died tragically as the result of an accident; his second marriage ended with the death of his wife only six years after they were married, and he had no children to succeed him. The homes he loved so dearly were destroyed by fire, and fate, not content by testing him so cruelly, dealt the final blow by depriving him of his eyesight. During the last years of his life he was totally blind. Yet such was Edward Grey's strength of character that he never became bitter, never repined, and retained his sweetness of disposition to the end of his life. He is an example and inspiration to all those who have suffered great loss and great sorrow.

Grey's family was a branch of the Northumbrian family who were distinguished from the other branches of Howick and Milfield by the name of their estate, Fallodon. Greys of Howick, Milfield and Fallodon have served their country and county in many different ways, as soldiers, statesmen and social reformers. In the early records of Northumberland their name is prominent, and one is named as an accomplice in the famous traitor's speech which Shakespeare used to such effect in Henry V. Chillingham Castle was the original home of this outstanding family. It was a Grey of Howick, whose name is for ever associated with the Reform Bill of 1832: and G. M. Trevelyan, in his autobiography of Grey of Fallodon, recounts the following utterance of Edward Grey on the subject of his kinsman:

> Oh, yes, I wanted to talk to you about old Lord Grey. People used to praise him and Lord Althorp because they were such fine fellows and passed such a good bill. They used to say it was such a pity that Grey always wanted to be away in Northumberland, and Althorp in Northamptonshire. But that is just the reason why they did so well whenever they were in London.

This passionate devotion to Northumberland was inherited even more strongly in the younger man, and in later years was the cause of much conflict in his life. After he entered politics and had to spend so much time in London, he was always longing for Fallodon.

Edward Grey always regretted the fact that he was the only member of his family who was not born in his dearly loved county. The reason for this was that at the time of the future Foreign Secretary's birth, his father was an equerry to the Prince of Wales, afterwards Edward VII, and for this reason his parents had a house in London. In his autobiography Edward Grey says, "I was born on April 25th, 1862, in London, and I have always felt that my brothers and sisters had the advantage of me in that they were all not only brought up but born at Fallodon." The Fallodon which Grey loved so deeply came into the possession of his family in 1775, when the daughter of Thomas Wood, then owner of the estate, married Sir Henry Grey of Howick.

Fallodon is a little way inland from the village of Embleton, which stands on the wide bay which bears its name. The first mention of a house at Fallodon is during the Commonwealth, when a merchant from Berwick-upon-Tweed, whose name was Salkeld, built a small house there. This Salkeld and his son planted a garden which was famous for its peaches, plums and pears, and it was said that "the improvements at Fallodon [*sic*] in gardening and fruitery are hardly to be equalled north of the Tyne". The garden and 'fruitery' created by the Salkelds was loved and cherished by Edward Grey; he is said once to have remarked, "You can never eat too much fruit." After Salkeld's day the house became the property of the Wood family, whose heiress brought it to the Greys. Rebuilt by the Woods, the house remained very much as it was until so severely damaged by the disastrous fire which occurred in 1917. Edward Grey's grandfather, Sir George Grey, who made his home at Fallodon, was Home Secretary in the middle years of Queen Victoria's reign. Politics were certainly in the blood of the Grey family. Sir George stood as Liberal candidate for what was then called the North Northumberland division, later changed to that of Berwick-upon-Tweed. The Liberal candidate managed to dislodge a Percy from what had until then almost been regarded as a hereditary Tory seat. This accomplishment was repeated when his grandson, fighting his first parliamentary election in 1885, again defeated a Percy. Edward Grey held the Berwick-upon-Tweed division until his elevation to the peerage.

Edward Grey's father, George Henry, did not follow the family tradition but made the army his career and saw active service in the Crimean War and the Indian Mutiny. Colonel George Henry Grey married Harriet Jane Pearson, the daughter of an army officer, and they had seven children of whom Edward was the eldest. Two of his brothers met with violent deaths: George was killed by a lion in Africa in 1911; and Charles, the youngest of the family, also died in Africa in 1928, after being attacked by a buffalo. Having no children of his own, Edward left the Fallodon estate to his sister Alice's son, Charles Graves, who subsequently sold it to the present owner, Colonel the Hon. H. O. Bridgeman.

Mrs. Grey was left a widow in 1874, when her eldest son was only 12 years of age. Colonel Grey died at Sandringham, and after his death his widow made her home at Fallodon with her father-in-law Sir George, who lived until 1882. It was at Fallodon that the Grey children spent most of their childhood, and there is no doubt that old Sir George influenced his eldest grandchild strongly. Edward Grey was therefore 20 years of age when he succeeded to the baronetcy. His education had followed the lines laid down by the Establishment: prep-school, followed by Winchester. By the time he was ready to be sent away to school the seeds of his character had been sown. He was above all a countryman; the country to him meant the woods and fields that surround Fallodon and, during his time at Winchester, fishing in the River Itchen. Fishing was one of the many country pursuits which he loved so dearly, and in 1899 he published his first book *Fly Fishing*, which is a classic of its kind. Fishing on the Itchen and on many Scottish rivers was to be a consolation to him in the years ahead, far away from the strife and turmoil of politics. Later Grey built a house on the Itchen which was called 'The Cottage', and there he spent many happy days, until his retreat was destroyed by fire in 1923. It was at his Hampshire home that he wrote his *Cottage Book*. Already his great interest in birds had been aroused, and this love for his feathered friends, as he referred to them, was to give him even more consolation than his fishing in the years of sorrow and loneliness which lay in the future. From Winchester Edward Grey went up to Oxford in 1880, where he was an undergraduate at Balliol, which now proudly boasts that Grey was one of its most illustrious students. The truth is that the future Foreign Secretary was sent down for "incorrigible laziness". At that time the Master of Balliol was the renowned Greek scholar Benjamin Jowett, and it was he who signed the Balliol minute book to the following: "Sir Edward Grey, having been repeatedly admonished for idleness, and having shown himself entirely ignorant of the work set for him in vacation as a condition of residence, was sent down, but allowed to come up to pass his examination in June. 19th January 1884."

For some time Grey was coached by the Vicar of Embleton, Mandell Creighton, who later became Bishop of London. How many times have men who later left their names on the pages of history had mediocre school and university records. Sir Winston Churchill is an example of this. Grey's first Oxford degree was his Honorary D.C.L. in 1907, and in 1928, towards the end of his life, he was elected chancellor of his old university. After his somewhat

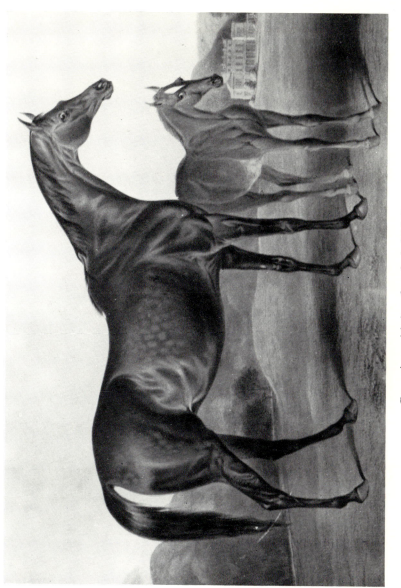

Beeswing with her first foal, Old Port

The last studio photograph of Grey of Fallodon

inglorious departure from Oxford Grey made up his mind to emulate so many of his kinsmen and make politics his career.

His ambition was to represent a Northumbrian constituency, and he was eventually adopted as the Liberal candidate for Berwick-upon-Tweed. Wearing the blue rosette of the Liberal party (blue is the Liberal colour in Northumberland), the young baronet of 22 set out in his dog-cart and sometimes on his bicycle to address meetings in his scattered constituency. He had no experience in public speaking, it is said he rehearsed his first speech in Embleton Vicarage with his friend, the future Bishop of London, as critic. Grey addressed his first meeting in the county town of Alnwick, where his Conservative opponent, Earl Percy, the Duke of Northumberland's heir, lived in the great castle. When the General Election of 1885 took place Edward Grey was returned as Liberal member for the Border division of Berwick-upon-Tweed. He was returned at every election he fought. It is not my intention to dwell on Grey's political career, that has been so ably dealt with by his fellow Northumbrian, the late G. M. Trevelyan, O.M., in his biography, *Grey of Fallodon*. In my opinion this is one of the finest biographies ever written, so fair is it in its assessment of Grey as a politician. I understand that at the present time some more research is being done into the life and times of Edward Grey. I doubt whether anyone, however well qualified, will ever equal 'G.M.'.

An even more important event occurred in Grey's life in 1885 than his election to Parliament. He married Dorothy Widdrington shortly before the General Election. The Widdringtons are another of the many old families of Northumberland who have such deep roots in the county. One of this family fought at the Battle of Otterburn in 1388, and, according to the "Ballad of Chevy Chase",

> For Widdrington my heart was low,
> That ever he slain should be;
> For when both his legs were hewn in two,
> Yet he kneeled and fought on his knee.

There is nothing left of the castle in which these earlier Widdringtons lived. It was close to the village of the same name which is a few miles inland on the road which leads to Amble, where the Northumberland coal-field ends. Dorothy Widdrington's parents lived at Newton Hall near the village of Newton-on-the-Moor, from where there are dramatic views of the Northumbrian coastline. Captain Francis Widdrington, a nephew of Dorothy's, lives at Newton Hall today, and it is due to his help and kindness that I am able to write so much about his aunt.

Edward Grey and his future wife met when they were out hunting, and it was a brief and romantic courtship. Dorothy was only 20 when she was married. I am told she was not a socialite in any sense of the word, and seemed rather remote from the rest of her family. She was deeply interested in literature, and this of course appealed to Grey. She loved outdoor life, and, most important of all in the eyes of her future husband, she loved birds. Many people thought her unapproachable and difficult to get to know, but those who did break through the barrier found a loving warm-hearted woman. She was the ideal woman for a man with Edward Grey's somewhat complex character. One was the complement of the other, and, although it is a much abused term, they were an ideal couple.

Dorothy shared his admiration for the poetry of Wordsworth, although her favourite writer was Meredith. Mandell Creighton had a great deal of influence on the young Dorothy Widdrington, and taught her to take a more tolerant view of other people's failings. I have heard that she was more at home, and more popular with the ordinary country people than she ever was with 'the County'. This may have been because she had no time for social conventions and the eternal social round, where she always met the same sort of people.

A picture of Dorothy hangs at Newton Hall today. She appears to have been classically beautiful and she and Grey must have been a handsome couple on that autumn day in 1885 when they were married in Shilbottle Church. They were the first couple to be married in this church after its extensive restoration, the new building having been consecrated in July. In the register of Shilbottle Church the following entry appears. "20th October 1885. Edward Grey. Frances Dorothy Widdrington. 20." The bridegroom's profession is described as that of baronet. Had Dorothy a premonition when she told a friend soon after her wedding that all she asked of life was twenty years of happiness. Her marriage lasted for just over the twenty years she asked for. They were twenty years of hustle and activity when the House was sitting and of peace and relaxation at Fallodon and at the cottage on the Itchen.

It was shortly after their marriage that Edward and Dorothy Grey took up their study of birds seriously, and it was to be an absorbing passion with both of them. During these twenty years Grey's stature in Parliament was steadily rising, and he had every hope of attaining high office, yet all the time his loyalties were divided between the career he had chosen and his longing to spend all his time in Northumberland. It has been suggested to me by one who knew them that it was Dorothy's ambition for him that kept him from giving up politics and leading the life of a country gentleman. I wonder whether the life he longed for would have satisfied him intellectually. The unobtainable is so often more alluring than the reality. Grey could not have performed his parliamentary duties so well had his heart not been in politics.

As time went on and his responsibilities increased his sense of duty kept him at his post. Those were the days before Members of Parliament had salaries, and Grey was never a rich man. Perhaps it is wrong to say he chose politics as a career—vocation might be the better word. He was never a strong man and there is no doubt that the strain of office took its toll, and impaired even more his already failing eyesight.

In 1905 Edward Grey succeeded Lord Lansdowne as Foreign Secretary, an office he held until the collapse of the Asquith government in 1916. How proud Dorothy Grey must have been when her husband's twenty years of service to his country was recognized and he was the holder of an office second only in importance to that of Prime Minister. Fate only gave Dorothy Grey eleven weeks as wife of a Foreign Secretary. The twenty years she had asked for were coming to an end. Grey planned to have a few days at Fallodon at the beginning of February, and Dorothy came north a few days before him, to await his arrival. On Thursday 1st February Lady Grey decided to visit some friends near Belford and set off from Fallodon in a horse-drawn trap (the horse had been hired from livery stables at Alnwick), accompanied by Thomas Henderson, an under-gardener at Fallodon. As they approached the school house at Ellingham the horse shied, and, although it was said at the inquest that Lady Grey struggled to hang on to the reigns, she was thrown on to the road and her head was severely injured. I have also been told that the wheel of the trap caught the projecting trunk of a tree, but there is no mention of this in reports of the inquest. Another unauthenticated story is that Lady Grey was warned that the horse was 'fresh' and not to drive herself. With the passing of time the stories have multiplied, but whatever happened, it was the end of Dorothy Grey's twenty years. She was carried into the school house at Ellingham, where she lingered until Sunday the 4th, never regaining consciousness. A telegarm was sent to Sir Edward, who left London immediately by train, and he stayed in the room with Dorothy until the end, whilst every effort was made to save her life. King Edward even offered to send his court physician, Sir Frederick Treves. Nothing could save her life, and with her part of Edward Grey died too. She was the one love of his life. Tributes to her memory and messages of condolence poured in from all parts of the country, headed by a personal message of sympathy from the King.

I have beside me a leather-bound book of press-cuttings which has been lent to me by Captain Widdrington. There are thirty pages with press-cuttings pasted on each side. The Court Circular and the national press headed by *The Times*, local newspapers and many which are now out of circulation, gave the news banner headlines. It was a tragedy that struck at the nation. The situation was like a Greek tragedy; the wife of a man who had just reached the peak of his career to be killed in the country she loved so dearly and where she had been born. The *Alnwick Guardian* had a supplement and a photograph of Dorothy framed in black. She was only 41. The inquest was held at Fallodon, where her body lay with a bunch of snowdrops on her breast. The sun was shining, and through the open window the squirrels came in as usual to fetch the nuts from their box. Dorothy Grey's body was taken from Fallodon by special train to Darlington, where she was cremated. Her ashes were scattered in the woods at Fallodon.

Sir Edward Grey returned to London immediately after the funeral and flung himself into work in an effort to forget, something he was never able to do. Dorothy was beside him in spirit to the end of his life. He made a garden to her memory in the grounds at Fallodon, and it is called Dorothy's garden to this day.

The ten years which lay ahead of Grey as Foreign Secretary were some of the most momentous in our history. The threat of war with Germany was already hanging over Europe, and the office of Foreign Secretary was not an easy one. In 1912 Sir Edward Grey was created a Knight of the Garter by George V, who succeeded his father in 1910. The Garter is the most ancient order of chivalry and a much coveted honour. Many times during these years of crisis Grey considered resignation and retirement, but the thought of going back to Fallodon without Dorothy must have been unbearable. Finally in June 1914, when only the most optimistic and peace-loving hoped that a war with Germany could be avoided, the assassination of the Archduke Francis Ferdinand, the heir to the Austrian-Hungarian throne, brought matters to a head.

Edward Grey, to use a contradictory term, fought for peace until the final hour. It is not within my province to assess his achievements as a Foreign Secretary, but to state facts, and when war was declared no man supported his country more than Sir Edward Grey. Some of his critics say that he did not go abroad enough but relied on the reports which were brought to him; he did, in fact, hate foreign travel and no Foreign Secretary ever travelled less in modern times, but he was aware of all that was going on, and was an indefatigable worker. His eyesight was steadily deteriorating, and he must have longed to give up, but he never did; yet perhaps in some ways he was relieved when the Asquith government was defeated and succeeded by that of Lloyd George in 1916. It had taken a World War to make him a free man to return to his beloved Fallodon. King George offered Sir Edward an earldom, which he refused. It was so typical of the humility of the man. Sir Edward said he already had a kinsman, Grey of Howick, who was an earl, and he would rather accept the lower rank of Viscount, and so he became Viscount Grey of Fallodon. It must have been a lonely homecoming, but he never complained, and his friends were delighted to stay with him. He had in Mr. Herbert and his sister stalwart helpers, and his staff at Fallodon were devoted to him. I have talked to two people who worked for him, and their admiration is unbounded.

Fate still had more blows in store for this indomitable man, when in 1917 most of his beloved home in Northumberland was destroyed by fire. Undaunted he set about rebuilding Fallodon, this time without a third storey. It is a 'rose-brick' house set in beech woods, and the mile-long avenue from the gates is flanked

by trees which form a guard of honour. Here at Fallodon he had
special ponds constructed for his ducks of which he had numerous
varieties. From 1916 until his death in 1933 he spent most of his
time at Fallodon. His longest absence from home was when he
went to the United States on behalf of the League of Nations. He
was too ill and his sight was too bad for him to take any active part
in the affairs of the Liberal Party, but he always retained his
interest in world affairs, and for as long as possible struggled to
read the newspapers. No longer when he climbed Ros Castle
could he see the sea and the heather, nor the Cheviot hills he loved
so much, but he still climbed to the summit and had a mental
picture of his favourite view in all Northumberland. During these
years as his sight and health grew worse Grey found consolation in
his birds and squirrels. He would talk about them for hours, and
the mealtimes of the birds, I have been told, were more important
than those of his guests. No one can ever have loved nature more
than Grey of Fallodon. He had strong religious convictions, and
he always maintained that good would prevail.

> All things bright and beautiful,
> All creatures great and small,
> All things wise and wonderful,
> The Lord God made them all.

Edward Grey lived by this conception of nature. He would
smile, could he know that a racehorse has been named 'Grey of
Fallodon' (it is a chestnut) and that it ran in the Northumberland
Plate of 1965. Grey once said that he had only bet on a horse once,
and he never did it again because it won!

In 1922 a greater consolation came into his life; he married an
old family friend, Pamela, Lady Glenconner. This was in no
sense a substitute for the twenty years of perfect happiness he had
enjoyed with Dorothy, nor did it mean he would ever forget her.
Lady Glenconner and he were both lonely elderly people, and for
six years they gave each other companionship. They each kept
their own establishments, and it was a most satisfactory relation-
ship. In those six years of his second marriage, when he was
practically blind, Grey dictated to Pamela his incomparable study
of bird life *The Charm of Birds*. Published in 1927 by Hodder and
Stoughton, it ran into fourteen editions and is still in print. It
seemed as though Fate never tired of dealing Grey blows, for

Pamela died in 1926, and he was alone again. Grey must have had great inner resources to be able to rise above the tragedies and misfortunes which haunted him in his personal life, otherwise it would have been so easy to indulge in self-pity. This he never did, and as an old man he still had a great deal of the small boy in him; he loved fun and simple pleasures. One of his great joys, in which his visitors had to take part, was to stand at the level-crossing at Fallodon as the The Flying Scotsman went thundering by. He once dragged his guests away from a tea party at Bamburgh Castle to see 'The Scottie' as the old steam train was affectionately called. 'The Scottie' is now in America, and Fallodon is no longer a halt as it was until 1934.

I have talked to so many different people who knew or remember Grey, and the verdict is unanimous: he was not only a great gentleman, he was a gentle man. Grey the politician may have his critics, but never Grey the man. It is given to few human beings to inspire such admiration and devotion as did Grey of Fallodon. Public life showered him with honours, yet he remained essentially simple at heart. He grew more frail with the years, and all his life centred round Fallodon, and it was there that he died in the Beech Room, on 7th September 1933. His ashes were placed beside those of Dorothy, and the inscription on the simple stone reads: "Here among these trees they planted together are placed the ashes of Edward and Dorothy Grey."

His country honoured him by a memorial service in Westminster Abbey; tributes which came from all over the world honoured the statesman while his own Northumbrians remembered and mourned the man. In the church of St. Maurice at Embleton a simple service was held to say farewell to one of Northumberland's greatest sons. In the church a memorial tablet lists his worldly success and pays tribute to his sterling qualities:

In memory of Edward, Viscount Grey of Fallodon, K.G.,
born 25th April 1862. Died 7th September 1933.
Succeeded his Grandfather Sir George Grey as third
Baronet 1882.
M.P. for Berwick-upon-Tweed Division 1885–1916.
Secretary of State for Foreign Affairs 1905–1916.
Created Knight of the Garter 1912, and Viscount Grey
of Fallodon 1916. Chancellor of the University of
Oxford 1928.

A statesman wise, valiant, single-minded—A friend,
flawless and faithful,
Also of his first wife Dorothy born 19th January 1865.
Died at Fallodon 4th February 1906.

There is also a memorial plaque to him on the wall of The Foreign
Office in London, with a particularly appropriate inscription;

Edward Viscount Grey of Fallodon
MDCCCLXII—MCMXXXIII

By uprightness of character, wisdom in council and
firmness in action, he won the confidence of his
countrymen and helped to carry them through many and
great dangers.

Above this is the plaque in stone with a relief of Grey's head
facing left. It is by Sir William Reid Dick and dated 1937.

At Fallodon today there is a feeling of sadness, as though even
the house is still mourning a beloved master. The ducks have
gone from the ponds, and the birds are quiet in the woods. No
squirrels go to the Beech Room now for their supply of nuts.
When in the summer of 1969 I wandered through the woods and
gardens of Fallodon I was reminded of the two lines from Keats,
"La Belle Dame Sans Merci":

The sedge is wither'd from the lake
And no birds sing.

Below Dorothy's garden is another garden to Pamela's memory,
and a huge beech tree—which when in full leaf is a hundred
yards in circumference—casts its shadow over the grounds Grey
tended with the devotion of a lifetime. The trees and flowers
seemed to be murmuring,

Better loo'ed you canna be,
Will ye no come back again.

7

Harry Hotspur, a 'Champion' Soldier

Now Esperance! Percy! and set on.
Sound all the lofty instruments of war,
And by that music let us all embrace,
For, heaven to earth, some of us never shall
A second time do such a courtesy.

Shakespeare, *Henry IV, Part I*

So much has been written about Northumberland's Champion
(as he has been commonly known in the county) that very little
fresh material is available, and it could be said he has been
'over-written', yet it would be unthinkable not to include him
in any book on Northumberland. Many and varied are the legends
which have grown round this colourful figure of the great House
of Percy; Harry, known to posterity by his sobriquet of 'Hotspur',
from his impulsive disposition, for his spurs were never cold.
He captured not only the imagination of his own county of
Northumberland but of the whole country. This man who spent
most of his short life fighting was, two centuries after his death,
immortalized by Shakespeare. The greatest of English dramatists
was never unduly worried by historical facts, which were often
changed to suit the structure of his dramas. It is therefore difficult
to sift the fact from the fiction and to build up an authentic
picture of Northumberland's greatest soldier. In the far off
fourteenth century few records were kept, and reliance for information has to be placed on the chroniclers and ballad-mongers
of the times; whose views were often prejudiced by their personal
and partisan opinions.

On his own attestation it is known that Harry Percy was born
in Alnwick Castle on 20th May 1366. The father of the future
Champion was the first member of his house to be created Earl of
Northumberland, and so founded the Northumbrian branch of the

family. It is almost inconceivable to think of the Percys as ever having been newcomers to Northumberland, for so long have they played a leading part in the life of the county. The family came to England in the train of William the Conqueror, and made their way north by way of Yorkshire, where the first Percy mentioned in that county delighted in the name of Als-Gernons, meaning literally 'with the whiskers'.

In 1309 the castle and lands at Alnwick were sold by Bishop Bek of Durham to a Percy, and from that time Alnwick has been the fortress home of the family. It was in the reign of the third Edward that Warkworth Castle came into the possession of this family of Norman extraction who were to plant their roots so deeply in Northumberland. When Hotspur was born these roots had been planted for only fifty-seven years, but already the Percys had established themselves as one of the greatest families in the North Country. The mother of the 'Champion' was a Neville of Raby Castle in the bishopric of Durham. Raby has been described as one of the finest fortresses in England, ranking only below Windsor and Alnwick. When Hotspur was 8 years old—and for once there was peace on the Border—the Earl of Northumberland took his son to France with him, accompanied by twelve knights, forty-seven squires and 160 mounted men. Even for the turbulent times into which he was born Harry must have been a precocious child, as he was knighted at the age of 11, and shortly afterwards is reported as taking part in the Siege of Berwick. As he grew to manhood it is said he was short and stocky, his colouring fair, his disposition headstrong and he was always 'spoiling for a fight'.

Fragmentary though these descriptions are, Hotspur's most outstanding personal characteristic was his speech defect. That he had this peculiarity has been established by the chroniclers of the times, and so much was he hero-worshipped that Northumbrians imitated his way of speech. Some say it is perpetuated for all time in the distinctive 'r' of Northumberland, which can only be produced by those born and bred in the county. Only in certain districts in Northumberland, such as Allendale and Tweedside, is the Northumbrian unable to produce the 'Hotspur R' which is produced in the throat instead of by the action of the tongue. Certainly this peculiarity does not occur in any other part of the British Isles. When at the height of his popularity he visited London, Hotspur was cheered more loudly than the King, and the courtiers tried to imitate his speech.

When there was peace on the Border, a rare occurrence in those days, the Percys and their followers set forth to find trouble wherever it was brewing. Their hereditary enemies were the Scots and the French. On one of the expeditions against the French, who were expected to invade the eastern seaboard of England off the Norfolk and Suffolk coasts, Harry Hotspur was in command of the army which was to repel the invading force. The Percy marched his men to Yarmouth, and there they waited for a sight of the French ships. To Harry Percy the waiting period was unendurable, and so he and his men sailed to France and vanquished the French in their own country.

In his thirty-seven years of life he can have had very little time to spend at Alnwick, where building and restorations were proceeding. It is surprising that he even had time to marry and beget a child. The woman who was his wife for so short a time was a sister of the Earl of March, Elizabeth Mortimer, and it was in an effort to seize the throne for his brother-in-law Edmund that Hotspur lost his life.

Before the final curtain came down at Shrewsbury, Otterburn and Homildon Hill were fought, and Harry Hotspur wrote his name not only on the pages of Northumbrian history, but on those of the history of England. The Battle of Otterburn was fought close to the Rede water on 19th August 1388 and has been the inspiration of minstrels and poets throughout the centuries. The famous "Ballad of Chevy Chase", the tune which the Duke of Northumberland's piper plays today, is based on this bloody encounter between the house of Douglas and the house of Percy.

> It fell about the Lammas tide when the moor men win their hay,
> The doughty Douglas bound him to ride into England to drive a pey.

Without the walled city of Newcastle the Douglas bragged that he would seize the Percy standard and fly it from his castle of Dalkeith, a threat which Hotspur swore to avenge. The Scots pursued by Hotspur marched towards the Border, burning the village of Ponteland on the way. Over the moors they marched down to the flat land beside the Rede Water, but were unable to overcome the little garrison which held out valiantly in Otterburn

Tower. (Centuries later this tower was for a time the home of one of Northumberland's historians, Howard Pease, who held the opinion that the word champion is so frequently used in the county because of its association with Hotspur.) Otterburn was not a decisive victory for either side. Some writers say that in the general confusion and heat of battle, the English were attacking their own supporters. Earl Douglas died fighting in the moonlight, having had a premonition, so it is said, of his death.

> Last night I dreamed a dreary dream beyond the Isle of Skye,
> I saw a dead man win a fight and I know that man was I.

The inappropriately named Percy Cross marks the place where Earl Douglas fell. Until recently the cross was surrounded by trees, which, as they were becoming unsafe, had to be felled. Saplings were planted, but unhappily these have been destroyed by vandals; and now that another attempt to plant has been made, the gate which leads to the pathway from the road has been locked, another indictment of this age of vandalism. It is humiliating to record the fact that Harry Hotspur and his brother Ralph were taken prisoner on the field of Otterburn and taken captive over the Border by the Scots! Heavy ransoms had to be paid before the Champion and his brother were allowed to return to their own country.

It was not only in Northumberland that Harry Hotspur became a legend and a hero, he was at one time the most famous man in England. In those days life was cheap, and 'gentlemen' spent their time at the wars. Very rarely did Hotspur appear without his armour, emblazoned with the Percy Lion. 'Esperance' was his battle cry, and often was that cry heard on the Borders when war was a way of life. The Percys regarded themselves as above the law, and in this respect they were not alone. Quarrelling with John of Gaunt, they changed their allegiance on many occasions; and when he fought his last battle, Hotspur's one-time friend and comrade-in-arms, 'Monmouth Harry', was his enemy.

An old woman had made a prophecy that should ever Northumberland's Champion leave his sword at Berwick, he would die in his next battle. In July 1403, the year that his son was born, the rebel army was encamped near Shrewsbury at Hayteley, waiting for the attack of the King's forces. Hotspur called for his sword, which could not be found. Someone remembered it had been left behind the night before—at a little hamlet called Berwick, far from Berwick-upon-Tweed where Hotspur had fought when a boy. The prophecy was to be only too true, for on that fatal field, fighting against his one-time friends, an arrow pierced Hotspur's eye and his eventful life was over—though not until he had killed the King's standard-bearer. Nearly six centuries have passed since Harry Hotspur died, but his memory lives for ever in his native Northumberland. Percys still reign at Alnwick, the ruins of Warkworth still stand, and in the ducal town the Hotspur Gate commemorates this fighting Percy. Just as Harry belonged to his county, so does his peculiarity of Northumbrian speech. In Shakespeare's words are Hotspur's epitaph;

> The earth that bore him dead,
> Bore not alive so stout a gentleman.

In the barbarous manner of the times Hotspur's body was dismembered and his head was placed on the gates of York looking north towards Northumberland. Permission was granted to Hotspur's widow to bury all that was left of the mortal remains of Northumberland's greatest soldier in York Minster.

It is extraordinary when one thinks how difficult communications were in the fourteenth century and how slowly news travelled that Hotspur in his lifetime made such an impact on the country. He would have become immortal had Shakespeare never made him one of his principal characters. It is Shakespeare who owes a debt to Harry Hotspur not Harry to Shakespeare!

> No more, no more: worse than the sun in March
> This praise doth nourish agues. Let them come;
> They come like sacrifices in their trim,
> And to the fire-ey'd maid of smoky war
> All hot and bleeding will we offer them:
> The mailed Mars shall on his altar sit
> Up to the ears in blood. I am no fire
> To hear this rich reprisal is so nigh
> And yet not ours. Come, let me taste my horse,
> Who is to bear me like a thunderbolt
> Against the bosom of the Prince of Wales:
> Harry to Harry shall, hot horse to horse,
> Meet and ne'er part till one drop down a corse.
> O! that Glendower were come.

> Shakespeare, *Henry IV Part I.*

8

Collingwood, the County's Greatest Sailor

Pray, too, that we may worthy be
To tread where our fathers trod;
Bravely to fight for truth and right,
For Motherland, King and God,
Fortiter defendit triumphans.

J. B. Brodie.
School Song, Newcastle Royal Grammar School

When Nelson was fatally wounded at Trafalgar, the Command was taken over by a Northumbrian, Cuthbert Collingwood. I remember when I was a child reciting with great dramatic emphasis a poem by Henry Newbolt, entitled "Admirals All". This was my introduction to the greatest sailor Northumberland has ever produced, and one of the outstanding admirals in British Naval history. To me as a child Collingwood was only a name, but a name which fired my imagination, and I needed no encouragement to declaim the verse in which his name appeared:

Effingham, Grenville, Raleigh, Drake,
Here's to the bold and free!
Benbow, Collingwood, Byron, Blake,
Hail to the Kings of the sea!
Admirals all for England's sake,
Honour be yours and fame!
And honour, as long as waves shall break,
To Nelson's peerless name.

Many were the press-ganged audiences who had to suffer my outbursts of patriotic fervour!

The first time I ever saw the sea was at Tynemouth, where, at the mouth of the great river, stands the memorial to the man who became Baron Collingwood of Caldbourne and Hethpole in the county of Northumberland. His choice of title was due to the

94

fact that he owned a small estate at Hethpole in the College Valley. Cuthbert Collingwood was born on 24th October 1748 in the city of Newcastle upon Tyne. The site of his birthplace is where the huge block of offices known as Milburn House stand today. A bust placed in a niche in the wall of Milburn House commemorates the fact. The father of the future Admiral had the same Christian name as his son and was a member of one of Northumberland's many old families which had branched off from the parent tree. In future years when Cuthbert the younger pursued his pastime of planting acorns whenever the opportunity arose, he was in a sense illustrating the history of his family. The small acorn which grew into the mighty oak is comparable with Collingwood's career.

Cuthbert Collingwood senior was born at Dissington—which lies north of the Military Road about 10 miles or so west of Newcastle—and was baptized in the church at Newburn on the Tyne. He was apprenticed to a merchant adventurer and corn-merchant in Newcastle. When his apprenticeship ended the young man married a bride who came from Westmorland, and had the unusual Christian name of Milcah. The two young people set up house on The Side, and from there Cuthbert Collingwood carried on his business. Four daughters were born to Cuthbert and Milcah, and it was at this time when the family was increasing that financial misfortunes overtook the young merchant. Fortunately for him he had friends who came to his assistance, and by the time his son was born, the family appears to have been in fairly comfortable circumstances. Life on The Side must have been most exciting for a small boy, for in those days the quayside was the centre of the commercial life of Newcastle. The coal-trade was booming, and the Keel-men were plying their craft on the coaly Tyne. It was the world of "Weel may the Keel row, that my laddies' in." The small boy would watch the ships as they came up the river, and perhaps he was taken to Tynemouth, where in the years ahead his statue was to stand guard over the entrance to the river.

Newcastle Royal Grammar School is justly proud of the fact that this great sailor is one of their most famous old boys. When Collingwood was a pupil, the school, then designated the Royal Free Grammar School of Newcastle, stood in the Westgate, and the playing fields were where the Central Railway station is today. Young Collingwood was fortunate that during his years as a pupil the greatest headmaster the school has ever had was in charge. This man, Hugh Moises, rescued the school from a period of decline, and a contemporary wrote: "By great learning and abilities, the sweetest manners and most uniform conduct, he restored the school which he found almost deserted of scholars to a flourishing condition." Among other boys he taught who were to make their mark in history were John and William Scott, who later became Lords Eldon and Stowell. The memorial to Hugh Moises in St. Nicholas' Cathedral bears an inscription written by his former pupil, William, Lord Stowell. There is a story that when King George III read the despatch Collingwood sent after Trafalgar, the King exclaimed: "Where did this sea-captain get his admirable English? Oh! I remember he was educated by Moises!" A biographer of Collingwood, W. Clark Russell, whose *Collingwood; with illustrations by F. Brangwin* appeared in 1891 says:

> No youth ever profited more from his school. Probably when he went to sea his Greek and Latin were hove over; I find no hint of an acquaintance with those languages in his letters; but in general knowledge there was probably not a man in the service that could have matched him. He loved books, and suffered nothing but his professional duties to interrupt the delight they yielded him. He was perfectly well informed in what may be called polite letters, was a student of everything good in English literature, and had such an art in expressing himself with his pen, as brings many of his letters, in polish, sweetness of language, and archness of humour very close to some of the happiest compositions of Addison. His fine taste was the gift of nature, but Moises must claim the merit of cultivating and directing it.

Certainly in later years during his long absences from home Collingwood was a prolific correspondent. It is sometimes possible to come across some of the Admiral's letters; they occasionally come on the market and are snapped up by collectors. Unfortunately there are no anecdotes to tell us why this Newcastle merchant's son chose the navy as his career. The only connection his family had with the service was by the marriage of his mother's sister to a naval captain, who later became Admiral Braithwaite. Whatever the reasons were it was a fortunate day for England and the Royal Navy when young Collingwood

Typical north Northumberland landscape

The Grey tomb, Chillingham Church

Langley Castle in 1882, before the restoration

went to sea, where he served for ten years under his uncle. At the end of the first decade of his fifty years' service, he was placed under the command of another Northumbrian, Admiral Robert Roddam, who was not only a fine sailor but a 'character' about whom numerous legends have gathered. The Admiral's family was one of the most ancient in England, having lands granted to them in Saxon times. Roddam Hall is in Glendale, not far from Wooler, and the present head of the family is Major Holderness-Roddam. Robert the Admiral had a most adventurous career, and his daring and enterprise must have had influence on his fellow Northumbrian. Admiral Roddam went through all the 'colours' which distinguished the various ranks of admirals in those days. From Vice-Admiral of the Blue, he rose to that of the White, from there he proceeded to advance to Vice-Admiral of the Red, and from thence to Admiral of the Red, the highest on the list. The Admiral lived to a great age and saw Collingwood reach the summit of his career. The old man died three years after Trafalgar was fought, having been married three times, but leaving no children to succeed him.

Collingwood while still serving under Captain Roddam, as he was then, saw service in America and was raised to the rank of lieutenant on the day of the Battle of Bunker's Hill. From the American station the young lieutenant sailed for the West Indies, where he was commissioned as a captain, and it was at this time that he met the man with whose name he is for ever associated, Horatio Nelson.

After this long tour of foreign service Captain Collingwood was granted shore leave and in 1786 at the age of 38 he came home to Northumberland. He remained in his native county for two years, as he himself said "getting acquainted with his family, to whom he had hitherto been as it were a stranger". Out of Collingwood's half-century in the navy only six years were spent in his own country, surely a record for a serving officer even in those days.

When Captain Collingwood was 43 (in those days regarded as elderly) he married Sarah Blackett, and the announcement appeared in *The Newcastle Chronicle* of 1791. "Thursday, Captain Collingwood, of His Majesty's Frigate 'Mermaid', to Miss Blackett, daughter of J. E. Blackett, Esq; the Right Worshipful Mayor of Newcastle." Captain and Mrs. Collingwood set up

7

house at Oldgate in the market town of Morpeth. The house named Collingwood House still stands today, although due to demolition all round, it has become almost an island. To those unfamiliar with Morpeth the entrance to Oldgate is beside the Clock Tower, and the road leads on to the River Wansbeck. The gardens Collingwood loved so dearly are now part of the grounds of the Roman Catholic Church. Though an exile in the service of his country Collingwood dearly loved his family and his county, and in his correspondence he often refers to his longing for his wife and daughters far away in Northumberland.

The people of Morpeth are proud of the fact that the famous sailor lived in their midst, and two plaques have been placed on the wall of Collingwood House. To quote again from W. Clark Russell,

> All who love and respect the memory of Collingwood, think with interest of his house at Morpeth. He saw but little of it; but it was the home of his wife and two daughters, to whom he was forever sending blessings in the fond letters he addressed to them from distant seas. No sailors home that I can think of has such an atmosphere of pathetic association as this of Collingwood. His heart was always there; his thoughts for ever with his beloved Sarah and his two little girls—on the eve of battle, amid the wretched monotony of blockading, in the hour of decisive victory . . . from 1793 till his death in 1810, he was only for one year in England . . . In Lady Collingwood's time the country was open, and the prospect from the windows just such a picture as a man far away at sea would recall, and muse upon with delight and love.

Collingwood, like so many distinguished members of the services, had to make great sacrifices; duty to his king and country came first, and, though his heart was in Morpeth with Sarah and his small daughters, his duty was of paramount importance, and when the call came to rejoin his ship, Collingwood was ready.

There are many stories of his eccentricities, some authentic and some apocryphal, of the kind which always gather round a well-known figure. It was at Morpeth that Collingwood became so well known for his obsession with acorns. His pockets were always stuffed with them and his feeling was:

> If the country gentlemen do not make a point to grow oaks wherever they will grow, the time will be not very distant when, to keep our

navy we must depend entirely upon captures from the enemy. I wish everybody thought on this subject as I do; they would not walk through their farms without a pocketful of acorns to drop in the hedge-sides, and let them take their chance.

He was not to know that the time would come when the 'wooden walls' of England would be no more, and strange craft which he would not have recognized as ships were to form the Royal Navy. There is a story still told in Morpeth that on his rare visits to his family Collingwood taught his little girls to have no fear. Just as Queen Victoria was to say in later years that she did not know the meaning of the word defeat, the future admiral would not admit that fear existed. According to the somewhat macabre story, this otherwise loving father chose the drastic method of taking his little daughters to the graveyard of 'The High Church'—as St. Mary's is known locally—at midnight to assure them that they need never be afraid. It would be interesting to hear what the present-day child-psychologists would have to say about this unusual method of eradicating fear.

In the year 1798, when the Captain paid a short visit to his family, he wrote the following letter to Sir Edward Blackett of Matfen.

Here I am now, settled in my own house with as many comforts and sources of happiness around me as anybody could reasonably wish. We are all in very good health, and have constant amusement in the improvement of our children, who we brought with us from their school at Newcastle, and, who, I think will be better under our own instruction at their age than at school. The change of air and good exercise, for which I am indebted in great part to your good horse, has made me stronger and better than I have been for some time; and had we but Peace I could be content indeed. But I cannot in the present state of things suppress an impatience to be in exercise of my profession, and this will increase when the newness of my present situation wears off. There is nothingness in a sailor ashore at such a time that will, if it lasts long, weary me; but I rather think it will not last long. Our Morpeth neighbours are very gay and good humoured to us; but when I tell you the dining-room where we dined yesterday was ornamented with pictures of Tom Paine and Horne Tooke, you will conclude we have strange characters amongst us.

Tom Paine of whom Collingwood had such a poor opinion,

was the son of a Quaker corset-maker (a strange occupation for a Friend) who had a chequered career as a political philosopher and writer. After becoming a bankrupt he emigrated to America, where he became a political agitator. He became involved in the French Revolution and published a book entitled *The Rights of Man*, in which he urged the British to overthrow the monarchy. Outlawed from England, he died in poverty in America. He was elected to The Hall of Fame in 1945. The second 'character', who delighted in the name of Horne Tooke, also had a curious history. The son of a poulterer, he went up to Cambridge, where he gained a degree and was ordained as a curate. While travelling abroad he became involved with radicals and revolutionaries, and went to such extremes that he was tried for high treason; but on some technicality he was acquitted and, strange as it seems, became an M.P., but was excluded from taking his seat, as clergymen were then ineligible to sit in the House. No wonder a conventional man like Collingwood was amazed that his host should keep such peculiar 'company'.

The host to whom Collingwood refers was a William Burdon, who, although a Yorkshireman, had been educated at the Royal Free Grammar School under the great Moises. After leaving Cambridge Burdon came to live in Morpeth, where he embarked on a literary career. He had a versatile pen, and covered many fields in his literary output, from a study of Napoleon's character to poetry for children. After leaving Morpeth William Burdon built Hartford Hall, which stands above the river Blyth in Plessey Woods, and there he continued his writing. William Burdon was much criticized for what today we would call his 'Left-wing' views. He and Cuthbert Collingwood would have little in common.

This letter which I have quoted is very revealing. Did Collingwood realize how much of his real self he was giving away. He was the kind of man who could never have tolerated a life of inactivity, and he admits himself that he was already tiring of the humdrum round of life in Morpeth. Was he deluding himself sometimes when he wrote the many letters in nostalgic vein to his wife and family. I find his character difficult to understand. The conventional side of him was strong, and he wrote the kind of letter a loving husband and father was expected to write. Was he revealing the real man, or was it a part he had built up for himself; in the idiom of today had he created an image, and was that image what the public expected. In my opinion, for what it is worth, the sailor dominated the man, which was what made him the leader he was. That he loved his wife and family I have no doubt, but he cannot have known them well; there was no regular contact with them, and in his long absences, when his life was filled with action, they must have receded into the background. Forty-four years out of fifty is a long time to be away from home, and, though he always stressed his longing for Northumberland, he cannot possibly have known the county well. From May 1799 until his death his life resembles a volume of *Jane's Fighting Ships*. England was constantly at war, and where the Fleet was, so was Collingwood. In May 1799 he hoisted his flag on board *Triumph*, and after a dreary time spent in blockading the Channel against the French he was promoted to the rank of Rear-Admiral of the Red. Mrs. Collingwood travelled from Northumberland to visit her husband when his ship was in Plymouth, and he was dining with Nelson at 'The Fountain Inn' when his wife and daughter Sarah joined them. He described the visit in a letter to a friend which reveals him in a more human light. The letter says "How surprised you would have been to have popped into 'The Fountain Inn' and seen Lord Nelson, my wife and myself sitting by the fireside, cosing [*sic*] and little Sarah teaching Phillis, her dog to dance." There was one brief visit to Morpeth before 1803, when war with France was declared and Collingwood left his home at Morpeth never to see it again. In the following year he was promoted to Vice-Admiral of the Blue, and in August of 1805 (the year in which he became Vice-Admiral of the Red) chased the enemy into Cadiz, an act which a professional writer described as "an instance of genius and address that is scarcely to be paralleled in the pages of our naval history". The year 1805 was one of the most momentous in the history of Europe. Napoleon was master of the empire he had created, and like every dictator in history was sure he was invincible both on land and sea. Adolf Hitler in another age was to make the same mistake, they both reckoned without the British Fleet, and the rallying cry, "The Navy's here," was to vanquish the hopes of both megalomaniacs and destroy their forces at sea. Admiral Collingwood was second in command to Nelson in his ship the *Royal Sovereign*, and the commanders had planned their method of attack. So much has been written about Trafalgar that it is repetitive to describe that most famous of all British naval victories. Even today, when man has achieved the seemingly impossible and landed on the moon, Trafalgar is still incomparable, for daring, courage and tenacity of purpose.

Victory still lies in dry-dock in Portsmouth Harbour, and every schoolboy knows the famous last words of Nelson to his captain, "Kiss me Hardy". (These last words of England's greatest sailor have often been questioned. One suggestion is that in the noise of battle, it was impossible to hear exactly what the dying man was saying, and that the more likely words were "Kismet, Hardy". We shall never know.) It is historical fact that as Nelson watched his second-in-command take the *Royal Sovereign* into action he turned to Captain Blackwood and said, "See, how that noble fellow Collingwood takes his ship into action! How I envy him!" It was "Admirals All" now.

> Admirals all they said their say,
> The echoes are ringing still,
> Admirals all they went their way,
> To the haven under the hill.
> But they left us a kingdom none can take,
> The realm of the circling sea,
> To be ruled by the rightful sons of Blake,
> And the Rodneys yet to be.
> Admirals all for England's sake,
> Honour be yours and fame,
> And honour as long as waves shall break,
> To Nelson's peerless name.

Collingwood's epic battle with the *Santa Anna* is one of the most dramatic sea-battles; two ships intent on destroying one another, until the Spaniard gave the signal to surrender. The mizenmast of the *Royal Sovereign* fell, "she was so ploughed up and shattered, indeed, that whilst manœuvring to get ahead of her prize, her mainmast went over the side, leaving nothing but the tottering foremast standing". Nelson had fought his last battle and gone to "The haven under the hill", and now Collingwood, the Northumbrian, was in command. His ship was a mere hulk when he transferred to *Euryalus*; this was his greatest hour, his name was already history, to be for ever inseparable from that of Nelson.

When Collingwood made his despatch to the King announcing the victory, the official reply was "His Majesty considers it very fortunate that the command under circumstances so critical should have devolved upon an officer of such consummate valour, judgement and skill as Admiral Collingwood has proved himself to be; every part of whose conduct he considers deserving his approbation and entire admiration." Admiral Collingwood's reward for Trafalgar was a peerage, and he received the King's permission to augment his arms (argent, a chevron between three stags heads erased sable) by the introduction of "on a chief wavy gules, a lion passant navally crowned or, with the word Trafalgar over the lion of the last, while to his crest (on a wreath a stag at gaze under an oak tree proper) was added a second—on a wreath the stern of the *Royal Sovereign* in waves, between a branch of laurel and a branch of oak all proper."

His country showered Lord Collingwood with honours. Parliament voted him a pension of £2,000 a year for life, with reversion to his wife of £1,000, and £500 each to his two daughters. He was made a Freeman of the City of London, and given a sword valued at 200 guineas. Newcastle, the city of his birth, gave him a silver kettle bearing the following inscription:

The Gift of the Corporation of Newcastle upon Tyne to their distinguished fellow Burgess, Vice-Admiral Lord Collingwood, in testimony of their high Estimation of his eminent services to his King and Country in various Naval engagements, and especially at the memorable battle of Trafalgar on the 21st day of October, 1805, when he gallantly led the Van of the British Fleet into action, and having succeeded to the chief command upon the glorious and lamented death of Vice-Admiral Lord Viscount Nelson, completed the most brilliant and decisive victory over the combined squadrons of France and Spain. Henry Cramlington. Mayor.

He received the Freedom of the Newcastle Trinity Corporation in a gold box, and the Volunteer Infantry presented him with a piece of plate.

Lord Collingwood wrote to his wife:

Blessed may you be, my dearest love, and may you long live the wife of your happy husband. I do not know how you bear your honours, but I have so much business on my hands from dawn to midnight that I have hardly time to think of mine . . . I have such congratulations both in prose and verse as would turn the head of one a little more vain than I . . . a week before the war at Morpeth, I dreamed distinctly many of the circumstances of our later battle off the enemy's port, and I believe I told you of it at the time; but I never dreamed that I was to be a Peer of the Realm. How are my darlings? I hope they will take pains to make themselves wise and good, and fit for the station to which they are raised.

These hopes Collingwood never saw fulfilled. He died at sea on 7th March 1810, only five years after Trafalgar. Fate did not give him long to enjoy the honours his country had showered on him; he was only 61. His body was brought home to England and he was buried in St. Paul's beside his old commander, Nelson. A street in Newcastle was named after him, and there are public houses named 'The Collingwood'. His old school remembers him on Trafalgar Day, when the headmaster and head boy lay a wreath on his memorial in St. Nicholas' Cathedral. A contingent of the school's naval section of the Combined Cadet Force accompanies them.

There is a much coveted prize at what today is called Newcastle Royal Grammar School, the Collingwood Prize. It is awarded each year to a member of the school who has rendered most all-round service to the community. It is not awarded by the headmaster but by members of the school who vote by secret ballot.

> Many a name on the scroll of fame,
> Is the heritage of our land,
> Collingwood, Armstrong, Eldon and Bourne,
> Akenside, Stowell and Brand.

The history of the school says that it never produced a more perfect gentleman than Lord Collingwood,

> The chief who, at the hour when Nelson died,
> With dauntless zeal, the mighty loss supplied.

Flowers are also placed in front of his portrait in the school on Trafalgar Day. He was a prophet who is honoured in his own country.

The long inscription on his memorial in the cathedral recounts his naval career in detail, the entire eulogy is worth quoting as it throws much light on the character of the man.

1st. of June, St. Vincent. Trafalgar.
Sacred to the Memory of
The Right Honourable Cuthbert Baron Collingwood,
Vice-Admiral of the Red and Major General of Marines,
Who was born in this Town of an ancient family.
He served with great Bravery in the action of the 1st of
June, 1794, and bore a most distinguished part
in the victory off Cape St. Vincent in 1797.
In the memorable battle of Trafalgar he led
the British squadrons into action,
and pressed forward with a single ship
into the midst of the combined fleets of France and Spain.
On that day, after the death
of his illustrious Commander and friend, Lord Nelson,
he completed the most glorious and decisive Victory
that is recorded in the naval annals of the World.
He held the command of the Mediterranean
for nearly five years,
during which he never quitted his vessel for a single day,
displaying unrivalled professional skill,
and conducting many difficult and important negotiations
with great political sagacity and address.
At length, on the decline of his health,
he became anxious to revisit his native land;
but, having learned that his services could ill be spared
in those critical times,
he replied that his life was his Country's,
and persevered in the discharge of his arduous duties
till, worn out with fatigue, he expired at sea
on the 7th of March, 1810, in the 61st year of his age.
In private life he was generous and affectionate;
a pious, just, and exemplary man.
A monument has been raised by Parliament to his Memory
in the Cathedral Church of St. Paul,
where he lies by the side of the Hero
whom he so worthily succeeded in the battle of Trafalgar.
His Widow, Sarah, daughter of
John Erasmus Blackett, Esquire, of this Town,
and his two daughters
had caused this cenotaph to be constructed;

And after her death, on the 16th day of September, 1819,
it was inscribed to both their revered and lamented parents
by their grateful children.

Admiral Lord Collingwood's life and death were the epitome
of Nelson's historic signal: "England expects every man to do
his duty."

9

Doddington Church and the St. Pauls

Dorrington lands is bonny and Dorrington lads is canny,
And I'll hae a Dorrington lad, and ride a Dorrington cuddy.
Holy Island for need, and Grindon for kye,
Of a' the towns e'er I saw, Dorrington for rye,

Northumbrians with their unlimited capacity for mispronunciation have corrupted the name of Doddington in Glendale to
Dorrington, and this local form is still used in the district today.
The village lies under the shadow of Dod Law, which rises to a
height of 654 feet and overlooks the plain through which the
River Till winds its way. A clan which bore the patrimonial name
of Dodding came down from their prehistoric fortress on Dod
Law and built houses beside the well some time in the twelfth
century. Probably earlier than this a church was built; there is
only one pre-Reformation reference to the church dedicated to
St. Mary and St. Michael, and this tells us that sometime between
1157 and 1184 William de Vesci granted the parish of Doddington
within the chapelry of Chatton to Alnwick Abbey.

The de Vesci family were the original owners of Alnwick
Castle, this accounts for the grant being made to the abbey which
stood on their land. An agreement was made to the effect that the
vicar was to take all tithes of corn for the whole parish and all its
chapelries, the land at Doddington was reserved for the abbey,
but the vicar was to have a suitable house on it. Originally the
church consisted of only a nave and chancel with the unusual
addition of a west chamber the same width as the nave. Although
many alterations were carried out in 1838 by Ignatius Bonomi
and the chancel replaced by a new one, the church still has an odd
appearance and when first entering one has the impression that
everything is the wrong way round.

The first time I saw Doddington church was about ten years

ago when I attended service on Whit Sunday. Since then I have visited the church and village on many occasions, and each time have discovered something more about its history and the people who lived in and near the village. At one time the village was so important that when a Doddington man died at Belford, forty lairds of Doddington each riding his own horse attended the funeral. At one time a weekly cattle market was held. The last time I saw Doddington was in the glorious summer of 1969, and the smell of the lime trees which surround the churchyard was almost intoxicating. Like so many churches today the living is now held in plurality. I do not wish to appear critical, but I feel that something should be done to revive Doddington church; it is much too interesting and historic to be allowed to decay. No two churches have the same atmosphere and they differ in characteristics just as much as people. This ancient building has an atmosphere of sadness and brooding as though it is filled with nostalgia for the days when it served a live community. In the churchyard there is one of the many watch-towers which were erected all over the country in the days of Burke and Hare, when body-snatching was a remunerative business.

Doddington in common with many other Northumbrian churches suffered greatly in the days of Border warfare. In 1296 the land was laid to waste by the Scots, who burnt and destroyed anything and everything they could. (It is only fair to say that the English did exactly the same things when they raided Scotland.) So poor was the parish as a result of raiding and devastation that it was one of the parishes granted immunity from the payments of tithes to the king from 1353 until 1357. Four years does not seem very long to give the land time to recover. In the autumn of 1335 'Dorrington' had a royal visitor when Edward III halted there on his way south from Scotland. The bridge over the Till, which was mentioned in records as long ago as 1310, was washed away in the great floods of 1947. The bailey bridge erected as a temporary measure more than twenty years ago has never been replaced.

The district abounds in legends which have gathered round the county's best-known saint, the shepherd boy Cuthbert. One story is that Cuthbert was 'watching' or 'looking' the sheep on the summit of Dod Law when he had a vision of the angels carrying St. Aidan to Heaven in their arms, and that the Northumbrian shepherd laddie vowed there and then that he would devote his life to the service of God. C. J. Bates, the historian, always maintained that the lonely farmstead of Wrangham on Doddington Moor was the original Hruringaham, the home of St. Cuthbert's early boyhood. A cave in the district is known as 'Cuddy's Cave' (another example of the Northumbrian's mania for 'Northumbrianizing' words).

A memorial tablet in this little Northumbrian church arouses curiosity; the name of the family it commemorates, St. Paul, is not Northumbrian, and what was a Count of the Holy Roman Empire doing in this remote corner of Glendale? It was when I was collecting material for my chapter on Josephine Butler that I solved the puzzle. Josephine's grand-daughter, Miss Hetha Butler was able to give me first hand information. Her mother was a Miss St. Paul, one of the family who had owned Ewart Park since the eighteenth century and where Miss Butler herself was born, her father being George Grey Butler. The family relationships are so complicated that one needs a family tree to sort out the ramifications, and even then it is difficult; as in the case of so many of these families cousins have married cousins, and the same names occur over and over again. In 1911 George Grey Butler edited two volumes of letters and material relevant to the subject entitled "Colonel St. Paul of Ewart, Soldier and Diplomat". Due to the kindness of Miss Hetha Butler, I have these books beside me as I write. To do justice to this family about whom today very little seems to be remembered, a whole book could be devoted to their varied and colourful careers. In a book such as this it is only possible to give a brief résumé of some of the more remarkable episodes in the lives of the St. Pauls.

Horace St. Paul, "Soldier and Diplomat", fled the country in 1751, having killed his adversary in a duel. By present-day standards the cause of the duel hardly seems to justify pistols for two and coffee for one, although on this occasion the pistols were discarded in favour of swords. Young Horace St. Paul was insulted by an older man in the presence of ladies, and in eighteenth-century England this was unpardonable unless a fulsome apology was forthcoming. In this case it was not. The account of the affair is given in St. Paul's own handwriting, a copy of which, yellowed and faded with age is beside me. It reads as follows:

On Friday 24th May 1751 Mr. Paul [the St. was added in later years] in company with his sisters, Mr. Blackburne, Mr. Dalton, and some other Ladies, were at a visit at Miss Green's. During the visit Mr. Dalton, who as it appeared afterwards made his addresses to the youngest sister, took a snuff box out of his pocket, and was asked by her for a pinch of snuff. It is to be observed that his snuff box was the lady's own, and had been taken from her a few days before by Mr. Dalton, to prevent her taking too much snuff. Some time after she asked Mr. Paul for a pinch of snuff, and he gave her one. Some of the company saw that Mr. Dalton was affected with this circumstance, but Mr. Paul did not, for being ignorant of the connections formed between Mr. Dalton and Miss Green, he did not expect so trifling a civility to the lady could be a matter of offence to Mr. Dalton.

There is a great deal of 'padding' until at last, in the dramatic manner of those days, Mr. Dalton 'sprang' from his chair and tried to seize the cause of all the trouble—the snuff box—from Mr. Paul. The ladies by now were having hysterics in the approved manner, and the stage was set for Mr. Paul to 'call' upon Mr. Dalton.

The duel was fought in Mr. Dalton's house, near Grosvenor Square. There were no seconds admitted to the room, and swords were used—it is said these were 'mourning' swords, which had blunt edges. At that time when the Court was in mourning duelling swords had to be blunt. The more I read and learn of the ways of our forefathers the more astonished I am at some of their peculiar customs. Blunt though the swords may have been, Mr. Paul's was sharp enough to wound his opponent fatally. "Mr. Dalton, still pressing upon him [Paul] staggered and fell. Upon this Mr. Paul dropped his sword and ran for the surgeons."

A week after the duel Horace Walpole wrote, "I suppose you would not give a straw to know all the circumstances of a Mr. Paul killing a Mr. Dalton though the town that talks of anything talks of nothing else." One cannot help having a little sympathy for Mr. Dalton, his efforts to cure a young lady of the deplorable habit of snuff addiction having led to his death.

Mr. G. G. Butler quotes instances of other duels which were fought—one as late as 1826, which, according to him, took place on the beach at Bamburgh and was fought with pistols between Mr. George Lambton, afterwards Earl of Durham, and Mr. Thomas Wentworth Beaumont, an ancestor of the present Lord

Allendale. This affair does not appear to have been taken very seriously as they only "exchanged pistol shots". I have heard many garbled accounts of this duel connected with Bamburgh, and each time the names of the opponents have varied.

From the amount of research Mr. Butler did for his *Life*, I am inclined to accept his version as correct.

At the inquest on Mr. Dalton, the coroner returned a verdict of wilful murder against young Mr. Paul, who had already fled the country. His exile lasted for fourteen years, during which time he had a horse running at Durham Races, so he must have kept in touch with affairs at home. In 1765 George III granted Horace Paul a pardon, which is in the custody of the British Museum;

> Horatio Paul Esq;
>
> His Majesty's Most Gracious and Free Pardon unto
> Horatio Paul Esquire of Murder, for and concerning
> the Death and Killing of William Dalton Esquire in
> a Duel, and all Indictments, and Convictions,
> Outlawries, Pains, Penalties, and Forfeitures,
> incurred by reason thereof, and all such Clauses
> are therein inserted, as are usual in Grants of the
> like Nature. Subscribed by Mr. Sollicitor [*sic*]
> General, by Warrant under His Majesty's Royal Sign
> Manual, countersigned by the Duke of Grafton.

During his years of exile Horatio had not been idle and had already embarked on his military career in foreign service combined with that of a diplomat. To have killed a man in a duel had no stigma attached to it in those days. Already the family was in possession of various estates in Northumberland, as correspondence with his brother Robert reveals. They were even making plans to deal with the flood water at Ewart, which estate remained in the ownership of the family until the marriage of the last Miss St. Paul, who handed over the entire property to her husband George Grey Butler, the author of the *Life*. Ewart and its contents came up for sale in the middle of the present century. Especially to a Northumbrian the letters which G. G. Butler quotes are fascinating, bearing out how little Northumberland changes. There is a reference to a shooting party at "Mr. Ord's at Whitfield". Now this branch of the Ord family (without an 'e') has its name hyphenated with that of Blackett and is living at Whitfield—and still having shooting parties.

A few years after her son's return from exile his mother applied to the appropriate quarters for permission to prefix the name of Paul with 'St.', a request which was granted. I have no intention of going into the details of St. Paul's career as a soldier and diplomat, as it does not affect Northumberland; but as an older man he came to live at Ewart in 1787. He is one of the very few non-Catholics to have been created a Count of The Holy Roman Empire, with the added privilege that the title could be used by his descendants.

It makes exciting reading to follow the activities of St. Paul and other prominent Northumbrians during the threat of invasion by Napoleon's armies. In 1798 the Duke of Northumberland, who was Lord Lieutenant of the county, raised what was equivalent to the Home Guard in the Second World War, and Colonel St. Paul offered to make a contribution from Glendale to be known as the Cheviot Legion. There were four companies of Infantry of fifty each, and two troops of Light Horse. In 1801 the King granted the Cheviot Legion the prefix of Royal, "Horace St. Paul Esq." to be Lieutenant-Colonel-Commandant. (Sometimes St. Paul refers to himself as Horatio and other times as Horace, which makes it difficult at times to know if he is one and the same man. G. G. Butler appears to have had the same trouble.)

Horace (Horatio) St. Paul is the only convicted murderer I have heard of who ultimately had such a respectable and notable career. *The Newcastle Courant* published an account of an inspection of the 'Home Guard' held at Wooler on 29th December 1803, which is so informative that I am quoting it in full:

> Of the twenty similar bodies raised in Northumberland, with the exception of the Percy Tenantry and The Newcastle Volunteer Corps, The Cheviot Legion was much the strongest in numbers: and it received praise at reviews and inspections, the ranks being filled by a fine sturdy set of men. An interesting event in the life of the Corps took place on the 29th December 1803, when it was inspected by Colonel Ker, the inspecting field-officer of the district, and presented with handsome colours by Mrs. St. Paul wife of the Commandant. The standards bore a crown surrounded by rose, shamrock and thistle, with the words Pro Rege et Patria above it, and 'Royal Cheviot Legion' below.

The following towns and villages had companies on parade: Wooler, Lowick, Bamburgh, North Sunderland, Beadnell and

Mary Hollon, the ideal wife

Emily Davison's Derby Day

The Tyneside Show, 1969

Embleton, Alnwick, Felton and Warkworth. "Mrs. St. Paul accompanied by her daughter then drove up to the centre of the square in a barouche and four, in which the colours and standards were placed half unfurled, which had a beautiful effect; and from the side of the barouche Mrs. St. Paul with a very distinct voice and most interesting manner addressed the corps in an animated speech." How thrilling it must have been to the Royal Cheviot Legion parading in their home-town of Wooler. The Legion never saw active service, but no doubt had the occasion arisen they would have defended their country as bravely as their grandsons and great-grandsons did in the two World Wars, when the Royal Northumberland Fusiliers and the Northumberland Hussars fought in many major engagements. Both regiments have now lost their identity, but their history will be handed down to future generations, just as we today can read about the Cheviot Legion.

Colonel St. Paul and his wife (he had married, in 1774, Anne Weston, who came from Surrey) had three sons and one daughter. The sons all made the army their career. One of them, Henry Heneage St. Paul, became member of Parliament for Berwick-upon-Tweed division. When Horace, as I prefer to call him, first came north, his eldest child was 12 years old and his youngest two. For a few years he rented Tillmouth Park (now an hotel) so that he could superintend the alterations which were being carried out at Ewart. While at Tillmouth the soldier and diplomat kept a diary, and the following is typical of its theme.

Sunday 5th Oct. 1788

> We had prayers and sermon at home. Several poor
> people came as usual of a Sunday to tell of their
> illness, wounds, etc., and to desire advice; it is
> ridiculous to think, that having cured a few
> people with ophthalmic complaints by Gourland's
> mixture, which I take care to have prepared with
> uncommon attention, my reputation has extended
> itself in such a manner that people come from 10
> and 12 miles distance to see me for relief, not
> only for the eyes, but for complaints in general.

What was Gourlard's mixture which was prepared "with uncommon attention"?

Like so many of his class and generation Horace St. Paul was

8

a man of many parts, and among his many interests was that of self-appointed veterinary surgeon. In the Tillmouth Diary he tells us about successfully curing a horse which had a broken thigh. The horse was slung from beams in a loose box at Ewart until the break 'knitted' again. (I can remember when I was a child, a horse which my father had only bought a week before developed lock-jaw and it was slung; but unhappily in this case it was of no avail, and in spite of every effort the horse died. There was no penicillin then. This must have made a great impression on me, as although it is so many years ago I can remember the vet [it was Fred Croudace from Corbridge] coming twice a day to try to save the 'Ouston' horse. It was a draught horse which had been bought at Ouston near Whitfield.)

Colonel—or, as he sometimes called himself, Major St. Paul (could he never make up his mind about his name and title?)—fancied himself as an industrialist and established brick and tile works on his estate near the River Glen. Two of his sons were educated at the well-known grammar school at Houghton-le-Spring in the county of Durham, the same school where Bernard Gilpin, the Apostle of the North received his education. It seems so extraordinary that a family who were once so active in the county should be almost totally forgotten. Some of the people mentioned in the diary have descendants living in the county today. Mention is made of Sir France Blake (the then owner of Tillmouth Park), Captain Gifford Collingwood, Captain Orde, and Admiral and Mrs. Roddam; Collingwoods, Ordes and Roddams (now hyphenated to Holderness-Roddam) are still prominent in Northumberland affairs. Not only was Horace interested in local affairs; he was a practical agriculturist and was asked if he would become a member of what was then called The Board of Agriculture. He was one of the first in the county to experiment with Swedish turnips, or swedes as they are known, obtaining the seed from Mr. Francis Tweddell of Threepwood in 1791.

His last letters complain of his feeling very tired, and having his breakfast in bed, but he always refers to some of his many interests. At the age of 83 he died at Ewart, near Wooler, and an obituary appears in *The Morning Chronicle* of April 1812.

Colonel St. Paul who died at Ewart House in Northumberland on the 16th inst . . . passed his earlier years in the most active scenes of life; he entered early in the Austrian service [no mention of the duel!] in which he bore the rank of Colonel, and was Aide-de-Camp first to Prince Charles of Loraine, and afterwards to Marshal Daun. In consequence of the manner in which he distinguished himself under that celebrated General, during the seven years war between Austria and Prussia, he was created by the Emperor Francis I a Count of the Holy Roman Empire by patent with remainder to his children and their issue . . .

The obituary extols in the conventional manner the many virtues which the dead man possessed; his memorial tablet in Doddington Church is couched in more simple and appropriate language:

Sacred to the memory of
Horace St. Paul of Ewart Park
In this County, Esquire,
Created a County of the Holy Roman Empire
by the Emperor Francis 1st.
He married Anne
Daughter of Henry Weston
of Westhorsley Place
in the County of Surrey, Esquire.

ob. 16 Apr 1812.

Sacred to the memory of
Anne, relict of Horace St. Paul Esquire
whom she survived 26 years
she died August 5th 1838 in her 92nd year.

So ends the story of Horace St. Paul, truly a remarkable one; and I feel as G. G. Butler did when he wrote: "If the publication of this book should rescue from oblivion a notable Englishman whose life has nowhere else been written nor has his name included in any collection of national or local biographies, my main purpose will have been achieved."

I did not think when I went to Doddington Church the summer of 1969 that I would discover such a fascinating and colourful story. My main purpose in going there was to see a window which was given in memory of the brother of a friend of mine, and which in many ways is unique. The window is to the memory of Major Kenneth Storey Morton. R.A. (T.A.), 'Tommy' to his family, and was erected by his parents and dedicated on Michaelmas Day 1946, almost three years after he was killed on active service.

He was only 28. Major Morton's home was at Hetton Law, and he dearly loved the Northumbrian countryside, especially the hill country of the Cheviots. The stained-glass panes of the window are not the conventional biblical pictures, but are all symbolic of the activities and places 'Tommy' loved most.

The central theme of the window is St. Christopher, and, to quote from a description written by Major Morton's brother:

Nothing much is known about St. Christopher, but the story goes that on one of his missionary journeys he came to a stream where a little boy asked him for a lift across. St. Christopher took the child on his shoulder and set off but cried out in midstream at the heaviness of his burden. The Child replies "Marvel not, for with us thou hast borne the sins of the whole world." This is the incident depicted in the window. We chose St. Christopher because he is generally accepted as the parton saint of travellers and you will remember that certainly Tommy was a great traveller ... He also had a great love for the unspoiled countryside and in particular for this part of Northumberland and so you will see in the background the Cheviot and Hedgehope each with a covering of snow on top ... For the last six months of his life he had what was, I am sure, the most superbly happy job, of his own choosing, as the technical expert on Anti-Aircraft Fire attached to Coastal Command H.Q. of the R.A.F. This service is commemorated by the four-engined bomber, shown flying at the top, which has been chosen as typically representative of the R.A.F. in this war.

It is so appropriate that this window should be in Doddington Church, not only because of the love which Tommy Morton had for Glendale, but because in the past this part of Northumberland was a battlefield. Many a Northumbrian and Scot who died in those strife-ridden days has no known grave, no memorial to his memory, other than poignant ballads such as "The Border Widow's Lament".

> I sew'd his sheet, making my mane;
> I watch'd his corpse, myself alane;
> I watch'd his body night and day;
> No living creature came that way.
>
> I took his body on my back,
> And whiles I gaed, and whiles I sat;
> I digg'd a grave, and laid him in,
> And happ'd him with the sod sae green.

But think na ye my heart was sair,
When I laid the moul' on his yellow hair;
O think na ye my heart was wae,
When I turn'd about, away to gae?

Nae living man I'll love again,
Since that my lovely knight is slain;
Wi' ae lock of his yellow hair
I'll chain my heart for evermair.

*Scott's Minstrelsy of the Scottish
Border, 1802–3.*

The old and the new blend into history in Doddington Church. Its own history, like that of Glendale, has been a stormy one, yet it has survived the centuries of Border strife. The atmosphere of sadness lingers, yet it has an attraction which is difficult to describe in words. I should like to see it filled with flowers, especially on Michaelmas Day which is the feast day of one of its patron saints, Michael—and the flowers should be Michaelmas daisies.

I've seen the forest adorned the foremost,
Wi' flowers o' the fairest baith pleasant and gay,
Sae bonnie was there blooming, their scent the air perfuming,
But now they are wither'd and a' wede away.

*"The Flowers of the Forest".
Morven Collection of Scottish
Songs.*

10

Langley, the Restoration of a Castle

Galling the gleaned land with hot assays,
Girding with grievous siege castles and towers.

Shakespeare *Henry VI*

Langley Castle in South Tynedale has been described by many
eminent historians as an almost perfect restoration of a fourteenth-
century fortress. This remarkable achievement was carried out
by the late Mr. C. J. Bates, who was himself a historian of repute.
The original stronghold dates from the reign of Edward III, and
I have described its early history briefly in my book, *Portrait of
Northumberland*. It is entirely due to the help and information I
have received from Mrs. Neville Hadcock, whose Aunt Josephine
was the wife of Mr. Bates, I am able to write in some detail about
the restoration of a ruin to its former greatness.

That I am able to do this has come about in a rather remarkable
way. Many years ago when I was a child living at Haydon
Bridge, there was a dancing class held in the town hall. Most of
the local children attended these weekly classes, which were held
in the winter, and I can remember one of the 'bigger' girls was
Jeanne Le Pajolec, who lived with her aunt at Langley Castle.
This appealed to me as being highly romantic, and I recall the
thrill when I was invited to tea in a real castle. That Mrs. Bates and
her niece were French added to the glamour of the occasion. My
outstanding memory of that eventful day is that we had the most
delicious peaches for tea.

Later I was taken by my mother to somewhat more grown-up
tea parties in the huge fortress-like home. Mrs. Bates was most
hospitable, and these visits to Langley were some of the highlights
of my childhood. As my interest in history developed and my
knowledge of local history expanded, I was even more thrilled
to visit Langley when I heard The Derwentwater Story for the

first time. The ill-fated Earls of Derwentwater, whose family name was Radcliffe, also bore the title of Viscounts Langley. None of the family ever lived at Langley, as by 1608 it had fallen into ruin. Sequestrated after the Rebellion, it was administered by the Greenwich Hospital until bought by Mr. Bates in 1882.

The survey of Langley Barony 1608 by L. C. Coombes, and described as an overprint from Archaeolgia Aeliana 4th Series vol. xliii was printed by The Northumberland Press in 1965. It makes most interesting reading, especially for those who know that lovely stretch of country which is South Tynedale. Many of the farms mentioned are still there, and the names of the tenants are as familiar today as they were in the seventeenth century. A Ridley was at Chesterwood; he is described as a freehold tenant and his rent was 13s. 4d. This farm must have been of quite a considerable acreage as George Tedcastle of Tedcastle only paid 1s. 8d.

The writer is particularly interested in Tedcastle for personal reasons; she has vivid recollections of beating over Tedcastle for her old friend, the late Robert Allen. One glorious day was spent in October beating some turnip land for partridge, and ending up in the Lees Wood, torn and lacerated by thorns and bramble bushes.

I remember telling 'Father', as I called him, that I knew by the tone of his voice when he was speaking to me or the dog. His voice had a tender note when he addressed Jester! At that time Robert Allen had the shooting over Langley as well, and we used to go on Sunday mornings to see how the hand-reared pheasants were getting on.

As I write memories are revived, not always in chronological order, but all part of the pattern, that makes up the past. I now go back in time, long before I tramped the Tedcastle shoot with Father Allen, to a day when Miss Jeanne Le Pajolec was married from the castle her uncle had so lovingly restored.

This exciting event in the social life of the district coincided with the first visit of the writer to London. That in itself was a milestone in my life. I know I travelled in The Queen of Scots Pullman which no longer runs and that I was put in charge of the guard.

I have kept all the letters which I wrote to my parents, and also those which they sent to me, and in two from which I quote there are references to the great wedding at Langley. My mother's letter is dated 29th August, and she asks me to "pray for a fine day for the wedding" at which we were both to be guests. My Father's letter begins "My dearest Nancy", and after many details about all the pets at Lipwood Well, he tells me that "Mother is at Hexham, and she is seeing about getting W. Arnison's best car for the Langley Castle wedding, as Harker's cars will be all booked up, as a great many people are going." The letter goes on to say that Wilfrid, one of the dearly loved cats, is having a board with Lipwood Well printed on it, in case "you don't know the place after your visit to London. Heaps of love and kisses from Daddy."

It was on a September day that dressed in our smartest clothes we attended the wedding when Jeanne Le Pajolec married Mr. Neville Hadcock in the Catholic Church of St. John of Beverley in Haydon Bridge. Unfortunately I cannot find the order of service and the seating plan, which I kept for many years. The reception was held in a marquee in the castle grounds, and photographs of the wedding group were on sale in Harding's shop in Church Street. It certainly was the wedding of the year for Haydon Bridge and district.

From then on the paths of Mrs. Neville Hadcock and Nancy Ridley divided, and had I not written *Portrait of Northumberland* I doubt if we should ever have met again. It was in April of 1969 that I received a letter from an address in Berkshire, saying that the writer had just finished reading my book, and was I the Nancy Ridley who once lived at Haydon Bridge. The letter was from the bride, whose wedding was the first 'big' wedding at which I was a guest, and whose home at Langley was the first Northumbrian castle in which I was entertained.

Since then Mrs. Hadcock has sent me the most fascinating accounts of the restoration of Langley and her life there from 1902 until her marriage. With her permission I am quoting much that she has told me, some of it in her own words. Without her help I could not have written this chapter. On Friday 17th October 1969 we met again at Bucklebury in Berkshire, where Mrs. Hadcock and her husband live. It was a far cry from the dancing class at Haydon Bridge so long ago, when of course we danced the polka. Our dancing slippers were carried in embroidered bags, and I remember sitting on my mother's knee wrapped in a Shetland shawl. There wasn't very much heating in the town hall.

It was in the same town hall that I was drummed out of the Brownies for insubordination. Brown Owl sent me home with a note saying what a naughty little girl I had been. I had never walked from Haydon Bridge to Lipwood Well alone before, and I know I cried all the way. What my crime was I cannot remember; my guess would be that I talked too much! It can't have been so very serious as years later I was a Brown Owl myself.

My banishment from the Brownie pack was a case of history repeating itself. My father used to tell me how when he was a small boy he attended a 'dame' school in the village. The old lady who was in charge of this peculiar establishment spent most of her time reading aloud to the children in her charge the most horrifying stories from the Old Testament. This gave the small pupils every opportunity to get into mischief, of which the boys especially took advantage. One day Robert Ridley was so naughty that he was sent home in disgrace. He told me that he could remember stumbling up the steep hill from the village to Peel Well, crying loudly for his mother. Beside the doctor's house, Haydon Lodge—where many years later my friend Robert Allen lived— my father saw an old man with a long beard, whom he was quite sure was God, coming to take him away. He eventually reached Peel Well and the safety of Grannie Ridley's arms, who assured him that the avenging God whom he had seen was only an old man who worked on the roads.

Such was my father's terror that he never went back to the dame school, even though he was very much attached to a small girl whose name was Josephine.

In the years that have intervened Langley Castle has been a school. It is open to the public on Wednesdays in the summer months. It is described in *Historic Houses Castles and Gardens in Great Britain and Ireland 1969* as "Langley Castle, Hexham [surely this is a mistake and should read Haydon Bridge]. T. A. Bates, Esq.; Restored fourteenth-century castle. 1½m. S.W. of Haydon Bridge on A686rd. to Alston. Open May to September—Wednesday 2–7. Other times by written application. Adm. 1/6. Bus Service United 37, from Newcastle. Alight at gates."

This somewhat bald description does not do justice to the

achievement of such a wonderful transformation, nor to the magnificent views from the battlements. The castle is also available for dances and functions, and the first time I have been inside the walls of Langley since the wedding long ago was in 1965 as a guest at a twenty-first birthday party. That evening for a brief time Langley regained something of its past glory. The masses of flowers banked against the grey stone walls, and the sound of the band made one nostalgic for the days that are no more. Mrs. Hadcock's history of Langley's renaissance has been made available to the visitors who come to the castle. How satisfactory it would be if all guide books were as interesting and personal. It is obvious as she says in one of her letters to me, that she "adored the place".

The first part of Mrs. Hadcock's "History of Langley Castle, Northumberland", follows very much the same lines as mine did in *Portrait*, so I have omitted the first paragraphs. She says "When Mr. Bates purchased the Langley Estate from the Commissioners he set about the restoration of the castle." The Bates family originally came from Heddon Hall, which is only a short distance from the village of Wylam, where I am writing this. Before going to Heddon the home of the family was at Aydon White House, near Corbridge. Heddon and Aydon White House were subsequently sold. Mr. Bates was a historian and antiquarian of note, and in a paper which he wrote for the Society of Antiquaries in Newcastle, he said:

> Thanks to the destruction by fire so soon after its erection, the castle retains in an almost, if not unique manner, the essential outlines of a fortified English house, of the great days of Crécy and Poitiers. Had it continued to be inhabited it would surely have been subjected to all sorts of Perpendicular, Tudor, Jacobean, Queen Anne, Georgian, or even Victorian alterations, or additions, at the cost of architectural purity.

With this "architectural purity" of the shell to start with, Mr. Bates set about the restoration work, which was to continue without a break, until 1914. In the south-west tower, there were in perfect condition sixteen 'garderobes'. These were considered unique, and the best preserved in Europe, and although they were covered over when Mr. Bates built the beautiful oak staircase, and erected a glass roof to obtain light—as there were only two small windows in the tower—the actual holes of the 'garde-robes' exist, and go straight down into the original moat.

The History then explains what a slow and costly business the whole enterprise was. Mr. Bates too, must have 'adored' Langley to spend so much time and money on what to many people would be dismissed as just another ruin. The right kind of stone had to be found, and the stonemasons to carve it. The only window on the second floor to survive the destruction to which Langley had been subjected, dates from the fourteenth century. The stained-glass windows were all put in by Mr. Bates. The emblems are interesting. One depicts the patron saints of Northumbria: St. Cuthbert, the shepherd boy who became a bishop; and St. Oswald, formerly King of Northumbria, who fought at the Battle of Heavenfield. Another window on the west side, also in the dining-room, displays the family coat of arms. The large window in the drawing-room is of the fleur-de-lis of France, and the Royal Arms of England, surmounted by Tudor roses. The inclusion of the fleur-de-lis in a Northumbrian castle is explained by the fact that in 1895 Mr. Bates married Mlle. Josephine d'Echarvines of Haute Savoie.

Their first home was at Heddon Hall, but so wrapt up in the restoration of Langley was Mr. Bates that Heddon ceased to be their family home in 1898. It must have been a spartan existence at Langley for the next few years. There was no form of heating other than open coal fires, and most of the heat would go up the chimney. No bathrooms of course and workmen everywhere.

This marriage was of very short duration, as in 1902 Mr. Bates died suddenly, his work unfinished. His widow, undaunted by the enormous amount of work yet to be done, was determined to complete her husband's dream castle. This marathon task she accomplished, severely handicapped by the fact that she could scarcely speak any English—she and her husband had always conversed in her own language. Langley Castle, or rather the restored Langley, is as much a memorial to Josephine Bates as it is to her husband Cadwallader. That the restoration was his brain-child is acknowledged, but it was by his widow's tenacity of purpose that the dream became a reality.

Special permission was granted by the Pope for Mr. Bates to be buried in the castle grounds, and a Celtic Cross (a replica of the Derwentwater Cross on the Langley road) was erected. When Mrs. Bates died in 1933 she was buried in the shadow of the castle which by her efforts and those of her husband had become the "almost perfect restoration". Cadwallader Bates was a most versatile and gifted man. Educated at Eton and Jesus College, Cambridge, his family were colliery owners. He was widely travelled, and spoke eight foreign languages. In later life he became a convert to Catholicism, hence his great interest in the Jacobite Rebellions. Mrs. Bates rebuilt the chapel in the south-west tower and dedicated it to the memory of her husband. It was in 1914 that the chapel was consecrated by the then Bishop of Hexham and Newcastle, in August, at the outbreak of the First World War. At the end of that holocaust a service was held in this private oratory to give thanks for the Allied victory.

The window on the south wall of the chapel is to the memory of Thomas Percy, the 7th Earl of Northumberland. This Percy was born at Newburn on the Tyne and lived as a child in Prudhoe Castle, one of the many Percy strongholds, of which Langley at that time was another. Thomas Percy was executed for his part in The Rising of the North, an abortive attempt to put the imprisoned Queen of Scots on the English throne. The Langley estate reverted to the Crown, and was lost to the Percy family. It is ironical that the Earls of Derwentwater lost Langley in the eighteenth century for their allegiance to the House of Stuart and that the estate again reverted to the Crown until its purchase by Mr. Bates.

In 1895 Pope Leo XIII by a decree declared Thomas Percy '*beatus*', or blessed. This unfortunate earl's feast day is on the 14th November, which was the date on which he was executed.

Not only was C. J. Bates a linguist and an ardent Jacobite, he was one of Northumberland's best-known historians, and his works are still quoted. He did not confine himself solely to intellectual interests, he wrote a book about his great-uncle, Thomas Bates, and the Kirklevington Shorthorns, a breed of cattle which his ancestor helped to make famous. In time C. J. Bates had his own herd at the Home Farm at Langley. At one time the Shorthorns outnumbered any other breed of cattle in Northumberland until the coming of the Friesians, a breed against which the writer admits she is prejudiced.

Without the invaluable information given to me by Mrs.

Hadcock, this attempt to write so intimately about Langley and the Bates family could not have been accomplished. Part of the text I think should be described as told to Nancy Ridley by Jeanne Hadcock.

I have no hesitation whatsoever in including her "Life at Langley Castle, Northumberland. 1905–1926" practically in full. It makes fascinating reading, and should be preserved for future generations.

LIFE AT LANGLEY CASTLE, NORTHUMBERLAND
1905–1926, as recalled by Jeanne Hadcock

My earliest recollections of Langley Castle, when I was brought to England from France by my Aunt, Mrs. Cadwallader Bates, began in September, 1902. This was supposed to be only a "short visit", as my Aunt, who was also my Godmother, was so terribly lonely after her husband's death, in March, 1902, and she felt that if she had a little niece to care for, and talk French to, it would mitigate her loneliness.

I remember well, the long and weary journey from Annecy (Haute Savoie) to Northumberland, and the terrible crossing of the English Channel. Everybody was terribly sea-sick, including myself, and I was "comforted" by a horrid old woman who terrified me by saying that soon the boat would sink and we would all be swallowed up by a huge whale! This proves that children rarely forget their earliest impressions!

I soon settled down at Langley, though I remember well in the early days, how I used to wander in my sleep, down the front stairs to the front door, and try to get out. Then I used to wake up and make my way back to my little bedroom in the north-west tower.

In due course I had to start lessons, and a Governess arrived. Her name was Miss Brown and her father owned the Paper Mill at Fourstones. She was very strict and stood no nonsense when I pretended I did not want to work! Miss Brown was with us some years and then I had a German Governess who was supposed to teach me German, but I think she learnt a great deal more English than I ever learnt German. For some time I shared a French Governess with two younger daughters of Lady Anne Bowes-Lyon, and I used to ride over to Ridley Hall on my pony, twice a week.

My Aunt never tried to either write English, or even speak it very well, and for some time, Miss Brown, my first Governess, used to do all her correspondence, but as soon as I was able to read and write myself, I was given the task of writing all my Aunt's letters, in English. Some years later, I was told by the secretary of the Bedlington Coal Company, in which my Aunt was a shareholder, that my letters, written in very childish hand-writing, and probably, not too good grammar, used to cause much amusement in the office!

The staff at Langley Castle, consisted of a cook-general, wages £30. a year, which was considered quite high; a parlour-maid, wages £20. a year; a housemaid also, about £14, a year; and a "between-maid" who got £10. a year and whose chief work was looking after the 16 paraffin lamps used in the Castle, cleaning silver, and sharpening the table knives and kitchen knives, on an enormous "wheel-grinder". Each maid was given a black dress for afternoons, 2 print dresses, 2 aprons and two caps! The Cook, I remember best, was a very nice Scotswoman, called Alice, who was with us 11 years; and a parlour-maid, called Vera, who came from Allendale, and who still writes to me every Christmas! In those days girls left school at 13, and "service" was the only form of employment open to them, so they were quite easy to obtain. They all had bicycles and usually went to see their friends in Haydon Bridge on their "half-days". Once a month, the maids were allowed *one* day off and usually went to Hexham on a Market Day, driving there and back in Mr. Dodd's farm wagon, from the Home Farm. The *one* day of the year, which was always looked forward to, was the "Hiring", on *Ladyday, March 25th*. It was a great day for the young men of the district, as they stood in rows in Hexham Market Place waiting to be "hired" by the local farmers, for the Haymaking and Harvesting Season. They wore a special sort of badge in their caps, to show that they were willing to be hired. When the "Hiring" was finished, the day usually finished with a Farmer's Dance at the Corn Exchange.

The maids at Langley all slept in the small bedrooms off the newel staircase. From modern standards, they must have been pretty cold and bleak, although with walls *6ft. thick*, one really never felt very cold anywhere in the Castle. I certainly never remember anyone complaining at all.

We did have huge coal fires in the Drawing Room, Dining Room, Breakfast Room (on the ground floor), Library, and in my Aunt's bedroom,—never in mine. A lift had been installed in the ground floor to the 3rd floor, and this was used by the maids to take up the buckets of coal, or heavy cans of hot water for the Hip Baths, used in the bedrooms when the modern bathrooms were out of order, or if the weather was exceptionally cold. My Aunt used to get *10 tons* trucks of coal sent by the Heddon Coal Company, *free*, as in those days the Heddon pits were owned by the Bates family. The trucks were sent by rail to Langley Station and then carted to the Castle in the farm wagons. From modern standards, life was not really very comfortable, or easy, for anyone, as we had workmen and masons employed in the restoration of the Castle from 1905–1914, in all weathers.

The large kitchen on the ground floor, was always warm and comfortable and lively, the huge range always in use, the Sunday joints were cooked on a spit in front of a blazing fire, and twice a week the Cook baked wonderful bread, teacakes and scones. I can still remember myself sitting on the kitchen table eating crusty bread, hot out of the oven, thickly spread with home-made butter from the farm! In those days, milk was 1d. a pint, and butter 1/- per lb!

My Aunt kept two gardeners who looked after the large garden and greenhouses, two gamekeepers, but these were dispensed with when the shooting was let to Mr. J. Straker of Howden Dene, in 1908. There were also two woodmen, to keep the woods in good order, a nice old man called "Andrew" who was always available for whatever help was needed anywhere.

My Aunt never owned a car, for a few years she had a brougham drawn by a nice old horse called "Charlie", but when he died at the ripe age of 24, we only kept my pony, and I used to drive a pony-cart.

When my Aunt died in 1933, the brougham, and a very fine Landau were still in the coach house at Langley, and presumably, were sold later. The Landau was the one used by Mr. Cadwallader Bates when he was High Sheriff of Northumberland in 1898.

We kept a few pet Bantams at Langley for my benefit, and they were great pets, also a large flock of white turkeys. At Christmas each employee and all the cottagers, received the gift of a turkey, also the Parish Priest at Haydon Bridge, the village Schoolmaster at Langley, and the Sisters of the Poor. My Aunt also gave a Christmas supper party with an enormous joint of Beef, huge Plum Puddings, Mince Pies, drinks, etc., for the staff, indoors and outdoors, at Christmas. On Christmas Eve, the maids (although not Catholics), used to walk to Haydon Bridge for midnight Mass with my Aunt and myself, carrying storm lanterns.

We lived very quiet lives compared with modern standards. Occasional tea-parties, the Annual large Garden Party at Chesters, which we always attended, and the Christmas parties at Whitfield Hall, and at Ridley Hall, were our only distractions. My Aunt's one interest was in her beloved Langley, and she was kept fully occupied for years, with the restorations which were still to be done, after my Uncle's death, and, of course, the management of the estate. Quite a formidable task really, for a foreigner who could not speak, or write, very good English, but she had enormous personality and always got her own way!

About 1910, when the north-west Tower of the Castle was finished, the huge bell (called the "St. Cuthberts") weighing 6 tons, and dated 1617, which my Uncle had bought in 1901 from St. Nicholas Church, Newcastle, when they got the new set of bells there, was installed with a proper revolving wheel. It was always a great source of interest to visitors to Langley Castle, who invariably tried to ring it. On November 11th, 1918, when the news came that Peace had been declared, my Aunt sent one of the men up to the Tower, and a joyous peal followed, for one hour, and was heard for miles in the countryside. Some years later the same Bell was presented to Ampleforth College, York, by the present owner of the Castle, Mr. Thomas Bates, for the New Abbey. A handsome gift, much appreciated by the monks of Ampleforth!

The Chapel, of course, was a source of great love and interest to my Aunt. The beautiful oak Prie-Dieu were made by Hammers in London, the Vestments by an Order of Nuns in Derbyshire (the Altar Cloths were made by *me* carefully embroidered.) The Tabernacle was made in France, and the Crucifix and Candlesticks came from London. We used to have Mass said in the Chapel, once a month, by Canon Dunn, the Parish Priest at Haydon Bridge. He used to come to stay the night and then celebrated Mass next morning.

Every other year we used to go to France for a holiday, lasting about 6 weeks, usually in the autumn for the grape picking and wine making season, when we stayed with relatives or friends, in Savoie, and on our way home, in Paris, which I got to know very well; or we spent the time on educational tours, for my benefit! I still remember the lovely museums, Palaces and Cathedrals, and above all the beautiful basilica of the *Sacré-Coeur de Montmartre*, where I was baptized, when a few days old, and my Aunt and Uncle Cadwallader were my God-parents.

In 1914 we went to France for Easter, and did not return home until June, when the war clouds were already gathering over Europe, for the 1914–1918 war. When we went back in 1919, it was to a very changed and saddened France. The North was still terribly devastated and naturally the loss of over two million of France's Youth on the battlefields was felt by all.

My Aunt's sister had died during the war and so had her only brother. *Seven* of her Nephews, all young men, aged between 19 and 26 were killed, mostly on the Somme, and my only sister's husband was blinded at the siege of Verdun.

Lanercost Priory, Cumberland

The Tweed spanned by Rennie's bridge at Kelso

The Water of Tyne near the writer's home

Willow tree at Wylam

We went to France each year after this until 1926, when I married. After I left Langley, my Aunt became rather a recluse, and seldom went anywhere except to come to see us in Hexham, and she was devoted to my husband and the children, especially to my daughter, Josephine, who was also her God-child. I used to get my Aunt "companions" at various times, but they were seldom a success and never stayed long, as of course it was a dull life and there were no distractions at all. The two maids who were most loyal were the old Cook and the Parlour-maid, Vera, who stayed with my Aunt until her death in 1933. A new Gardener and his wife, by name of Stuart, were also very faithful and devoted. They remained as caretakers for some years at Langley.

My Aunt died on April 12th, 1933, after a short illness, and she was laid to rest in the vault, in the Castle grounds, where her husband was buried in 1902.

Jeanne Hadcock
(née Jeanne Le Pajolec)

In an old scrap-book I have discovered an article entitled "A Visit to Hexham and Neighbourhood" by John Robinson, Sunderland. It is dated 1918, and is an appreciation of the way in which the restoration of Langley Castle had been carried out.

During my brief visit to the South Tyne I often wandered around the delightful surroundings of Langley Castle, which is one of the few ancient castles in England that has not been disfigured by the alterations of modern builders. The extensive knowledge of archaeology and antiquarian taste of the late Mr. Cadwallader Bates, has retained the original designs of the fourteenth century architecture of the castle in his restorations.

Mr. Robinson quotes a verse of poetry by Mark Akenside which is appropriate to Langley.

> Would I again were with you, O ye dales
> Of Tyne, and ye most ancient woodlands; where
> Oft as the 'giant flood obliquely strides
> And his banks open, and his lawns extend,
> Stops short the pleased traveller to view,
> Presiding o'er the scene some rustic tower
> Founded by Normans or by Saxon hands.

Few people remember that Mark Akenside was a Newcastle man. He was educated at the Royal Grammar School, Newcastle upon Tyne, taking a degree in medicine at the University of

Leiden in 1744. This man from the North practised in London and was appointed physician to the consort of George III in 1761. He died in 1770. Not only did Akenside achieve fame in his profession, he also became a noted poet. One of his best known poems is "Pleasures of the Imagination". His name is commemorated in Akenside Terrace in Jesmond and in the School Song of The Royal Grammar School.

> Many a name on the scroll of fame,
> Is the heritage of our land:
> Collingwood, Armstrong, Eldon and Bourne,
> Akenside, Stowell and Brand.

Northumbrians have a great many people of whom to be proud on the scroll of fame of their county—this county which has more castles than any other in The British Isles—among them Langley is outstanding as an almost perfect restoration.

II

THE DISTAFF SIDE:
Mary Hollon and Elizabeth Rowell

Ladies all I pray
make free,
And tell me how you
like your tea.
—*Verse on old Sunderland Jug*

When I was asked in 1967 to give a talk on Northumberland at the Hollon Tea—or Feast as it is sometimes called—which was to be held in the 'George and Dragon Hotel' in the market town of Morpeth, I had no idea what such a function commemorated. The invitation informed me that there would be "A liberal meat tea", and my curiosity was aroused by this rather unusual wording. I immediately set about finding out all I could about the Hollon Tea. With the help of Morpethians, as the Morpeth people describe themselves, and local newspapers, I discovered a fascinating story. It always gives me satisfaction to learn more about my own county, and, being a traditionalist, I was delighted that a custom such as "the liberal meat tea" was celebrating its 87th anniversary.

The story, which reads rather like a fairy tale, began in November 1855, when Mary Trotter left her home in Newgate Street to become the bride of Richard Hollon, a chemist from York. The marriage took place in the old Presbyterian Church in Cottingwood Lane, and Mary was given away by her uncle, Doctor William Trotter, a bachelor, with whom his niece had lived since the death of her father in Burma.

The Trotters were a long established Morpeth family, Mary's grandfather having been minister of the church in which this memorable wedding took place for more than fifty years. Her father was Captain John Spottiswoode Trotter of what is described as the Madras Native Infantry, while her uncle, the doctor, was four times mayor of his native town. The bridegroom, Richard Hollon, became Lord Mayor of his native city of York. The marriage of Mary and her Richard lasted for twenty-five years, Mary dying in the year of their silver wedding. Theirs had been a supremely happy marriage; and when his wife died her husband wished by some charitable deed to perpetuate Mary's name for all time. Richard Hollon was not a typical Victorian in his ideas of how the woman he had loved so dearly should be remembered; instead of the conventional elaborate memorial so dearly loved by sentimentalists, he had the inspiration to found the Hollon Trust in Morpeth, where Mary had spent her girlhood and where their wedding had taken place.

Morpeth seems to have meant a great deal to Richard Hollon, Yorkshireman though he was. In the town hall of this ancient borough hang portraits of the one-time Lord Mayor of York and Mary his wife. Richard is wearing his robes and chain of office, while Mary is pictured in all the glory of Victorian fashion. She is wearing the dress in which she attended, as Lady Mayoress of York, a ball given by Queen Victoria. Judging from her portrait Mary Hollon seems to have been a well-built woman of moderate height, but so voluminous is her crinoline that she may not have been so—although it is noticeable that her waist is not the usual nipped in one, so beloved of women of her generation.

Unfortunately there is little information about the life the Hollons led in the city of York; scraps of information which have survived give the impression that Richard, in spite of his participation in public affairs, was a rather shy and retiring man. This impression is borne out by the fact that when the drinking fountain erected to Mary's memory in Morpeth Market Place was unveiled in 1885, Mary's widower did not attend the ceremony. This fountain is the only conventional memorial to Mary. Perhaps the memories of Morpeth were too poignant, and Richard felt that he could not face the places so closely associated with his Mary. The unveiling of the drinking fountain was performed by the then Mayor of Morpeth, Mr. T. Gillespie, and afterwards sports were held, which have now been discontinued.

In the same year that Mary died the first Hollon Tea was held in Morpeth at 'The Queen's Head', although it was not until January of 1881 that 'The Mary Hollon Annuity and Coal Fund' was established by the transfer of stocks and shares to the value of

£7,111 1s. 2d. to the mayor and corporation of Morpeth. The trust deed reads as follows:

> The principal purpose for which the Mary Hollon Annuity and Coal Fund is established is the payment out of the income of the same to 13 women and 12 men until their respective deaths, or until determined as hereinafter mentioned, of an annuity of £10 a year apiece. The money to be paid quarterly and on November 5th the Corporation shall provide at some good hotel in Morpeth a liberal meat tea for the annuitants, in remembrance of the donor's marriage and shall use their best endeavours, to procure some Protestant clergyman or minister of the Gospel or some other suitable person to deliver an address to them on the occasion.

The deed goes on to say that any surplus was to provide a gift of coals "amongst such poor and deserving persons residing within the said borough of Morpeth or Township of Buller's Green in such proportion as the Corporation think possible". Originally the money was invested in coal, iron and railways, all now nationalized industries resulting in a decrease in revenue.

As so often happens with bequests administered by public bodies, there was criticism, and the public, or sections of it, demanded more details. In the case of The Hollon Trust the dissatisfaction reached such a pitch in 1894 that *The Morpeth Herald* published in full the text of the trust. The newspapers were nothing if not dramatic in Victorian days, and the introduction which appeared before the copy of the deed is worth reproducing. *The Herald* is dated 13th January 1894 (thirteen years after Richard Hollon had entered into his agreement with the Corporation of Morpeth):

The Hollon Deed Trust.
Full Text and Contents
The People No Longer in Ignorance.
(Supplied by our Invisible Reporter)

We made an offer to print in our columns, free of charge, the full text and contents of the Mary Hollon Coal and Annuity Deed, if the Town Council would authorize the Town Clerk to lend us the draft copy. The offer was unheeded, although the burgesses as co-trustees with the corporation had a right to know. On whose side misrepresentation lies we leave the public to judge, but unlike the Town Council, having nothing to gain by keeping the burgesses in ignorance of the truth we have been able to obtain a copy of the

Trust Deed from an independent source, and here print below the full details so that 'he who runs may read'. The burgesses and public generally after reading the Deed will readily perceive why it was considered advisable, on the part of some of our local legislators, that ignorance on the subject should prevail.

The full text of the deed follows, together with a list of the first annuitants. What accusations were levelled at the legislators the "invisible" reporter does not say; perhaps the law of libel restrained him. At the end of the deed is a valuation of the trust, with a tail-piece to the effect that no allowance has been made for income tax because the same is recoverable every year! How easy it must have been to audit books in 1894. Whatever caused *The Morpeth Herald* to obtain a copy of the deed from "independent sources" and to challenge the "legislator" must have had a satisfactory conclusion, as many bequests have been given to the trust and so the original capital has increased. It is due to the present proprietors of this local newspaper that I have been able to quote so much in full; they very kindly supplied me with a reprint of the report, and to them I am most grateful.

A recent edition of *The Herald* giving an account of the 1967 Tea quotes Alderman Alfred Appleby, J.P., Treasurer of the Trust, as saying that when he became a member of the council more than thirty years before there were enough funds to provide 250 tons of coal, which was then 18s. a ton. Today the annuitants receive £10., 5 hundredweights of coal, which is delivered to them, and they can order a joint of meat from their own butcher and send the bill to the trustees. To qualify as an annuitant the rules are that a man or woman must be more than 60 years of age and have lived in Morpeth or Buller's Green for at least fifteen years. Then comes the sting. The donor lays down that applicants for his generosity must be of "good, honest, sober and of good moral character, and shall not have been an inmate of any Union Workhouse, nor received outdoor relief from the poor rate". Should the successful man or woman come up to the standards laid down and be accepted they are not automatically "life" members. The corporation reserves the right to withdraw the annuity and other perquisites if the annuitants 'misbehave' themselves. It would be interesting to know whether this power has at any time been exercised, and what constitutes 'misbehaviour'.

When the first tea was held in 1880 the address was given by the

Presbyterian minister, the Reverend J. Anderson, who had officiated at Richard and Mary's wedding twenty-five years before. No mention is ever made of a family, so one assumes that this outstandingly happy marriage was childless. This no doubt accentuated Richard's resolve that his wife's name should have immortality. This devotion to Mary's memory is reminiscent of the sentiments expressed in Elizabeth Barrett Browning's incomparable sonnet:

> How do I love thee? Let me count the ways.
> I love thee to the depth and breadth and height
> My soul can reach, when feeling out of sight
> For the ends of being and ideal Grace.
> I love thee to the level of every day's
> Most quiet need, by sun and candlelight.
> I love thee freely, as men strive for Right;
> I love thee purely, as they turn from Praise.
> I love thee with the passion put to use
> In my old griefs, and with my childhood's faith.
> I love thee with a love I seemed to lose
> With my lost saints,—I love thee with the breath,
> Smiles, tears, of all my life!—and, if God choose,
> I shall but love thee better after death.

One can only hope and trust that despite the Welfare State, and the so-called march of progress, the Hollon Tea will survive, not only to perpetuate an ideal marriage but to bring a little comfort and happiness into somewhat drab lives. Only a decade ahead will see the centenary of Richard Hollon's bequest, and, if I am 'spared', as it is said in Northumberland, I hope I shall read in *The Morpeth Herald* that yet another company of annuitants sat down to a 'liberal' meat tea in a Morpeth hotel.

What changes Mary would see in her home town today. Mercifully many of the familiar places she knew so well are still standing and recognizable. Telford's bridge still spans the Wansbeck, although soon much of the traffic will be diverted on to the new stretch of road which is to by-pass the town. In many ways this is a change for the better, as the narrow streets of Morpeth cannot cope with the volume of traffic heading north and south. The clock Mary gave to St. George's church still marks the passage of time, although now it is electrically operated. The inscription Mary chose, "Redeem the Time", has an even stronger message today than it had in the nineteenth century. A plaque also given by Mary is within the church and is to the memory of her uncle. Although the greater part of her life was spent in York, the city of her adoption, her love for Morpeth remained steadfast. Morpeth can only have had happy memories for her. The fatherless child must have found in her bachelor uncle a kind and understanding guardian.

I am delighted that I was asked to be the guest-speaker at the 87th anniversary of the Hollon Tea. Had I not been I doubt if I should ever have heard of the enchanting love story of Richard and Mary, or enjoyed a 'liberal' meat tea in 'The George and Dragon'. The mayor and corporation of Morpeth were there in full strength, and the address was given by the Reverend Douglas Wood, minister of the Congregational Church. (Richard Hollon stressed that an address not a sermon should be given.) Towards the end of the feast, and just before I was due to speak, we were all, civic dignitaries and annuitants, given a glass of whisky. Northumbrians always refer to a 'glass' of intoxicating liquor, never a tot or a dram; this must give the uninitiated the impression that we are hard drinkers in Northumberland. The toast was of course to Richard and Mary Hollon, the bride and bridegroom of 112 years ago. As we sat down after the toast, a very elderly annuitant remained standing, and announced in the broadest of broad Northumbrian that, having had all she could get, she was "gannin' hyem (home) before the speechifying". I have always maintained that it is impossible ever to have a swollen head in 'wor' county; Northumbrians say what they think, despite the consequences. Being a dyed-in-the-wool Northumbrian myself I had every sympathy with the lady. A speaker from the South of England might not have understood. 'Speechifying' the old lady may not have approved, but I am sure she was proud to be one of the select band of annuitants who drank to the memory of Richard and Mary Hollon.

No two women's lives can be greater contrasts than those of Mary Hollon and Elizabeth Rowell, the Bardon Mill centenarian. The former died after twenty-five years of marriage, while the latter survived her husband by seventy-five, which must be almost a record. One was born abroad, the other died in the Northumbrian farmhouse of her birth. To the north of Bardon Mill, clinging to the high ground which overlooks the valley of the South Tyne, are the hamlets of Thorngrafton and West End Town. One house at West End Town stands out conspicuously from the grey stone of the district: The White House. It stands aloof from its surroundings in its own grounds wearing a rather superior air. Here in the year 1821 was born Elizabeth Bell, the eldest child of prosperous farmers, who lived to the remarkable age of 100 and died in the house where she was born. Elizabeth's mother was a Woodman of Whitechapel, a farm standing between Haydon Bridge and Bardon Mill, and was therefore a first cousin of my grandfather, Matthew Ridley.

As a child I was told many stories about this, as I imagined, rather fearsome old lady whom I never saw, as by the time I was born "your grandfather's" cousin was "bed-ridden". I never really understood what the curious expression 'bed-ridden' meant, and for some reason known only to myself I associated the old lady with the fairy tale of Red Riding Hood and the Wolf. It is only within the last few years that I have traced the story of this South Tyne centenarian.

Elizabeth Bell was the eldest of three children. Her sister Margaret was born at The White House in 1823; while the youngest member of the family, John, was born at Whinnetley, which is a farm in the parish of Haydon. The records of the Bell children's births were entered, according to the custom of the times, in the family Bible. Elizabeth spent the whole of her hundred years in the county of her birth. Until her marriage her home was Bardon Mill; for her brief period of married life she lived in Hexham; as a widow she lived in the city of Newcastle before making her permanent home at The White House. In her nineteenth year Elizabeth Bell was married to Soulsby Rowell, who is described as a wine and spirit merchant of Hexham. Old records and directories of Northumberland list many Rowells in Hexham and the Stamfordham districts, and a Soulsby was a tailor in Stamfordham village. This Soulsby may have been related to the Rowells, hence the somewhat unusual christian name, which was also given to Elizabeth's son. After only six years of marriage Soulsby Rowell died and left Elizabeth a widow with two small children. Her widowhood was to last for seventy-five years.

Elizabeth Rowell must have been a woman of strong character;

there was no returning to the parental home with her babies as many a woman of her day would have done. Instead she moved to the city of Newcastle, where there were better educational facilities than in the market town of Hexham. The widow must also have been well provided for, as no expense seems to have been spared to educate her children, especially of course her son. Higher education for women was still in the future when Elizabeth Rowell was a young woman. Annie, the elder of the Rowell children, grew up to be the typical dutiful daughter of so many middle-class families. Although she survived her mother by a few years, she never seems to have had a life of her own and devoted herself to the care of the much stronger-willed woman. I cannot help thinking that it was this unselfish devotion which played a great part in keeping Mrs. Rowell alive for a hundred years. Needless to say, Annie never married. If any young man appeared to be interested I am sure he would not be encouraged by Mama.

Soulsby, being a man, escaped from the maternal clutches and made a distinguished career for himself abroad. How garbled were the versions told to the young when I was a child. Soulsby was not considered respectable by his relations because he had lived for so much of his life in France. The French for some reason were not considered 'nice', and I was told not to ask questions about anyone who deserted his country for the temptations of Continental life. The truth is quite different, and John Soulsby Rowell's career was not only meritorious but conventionally respectable.

Soulsby was educated at Doctor Bruce's Academy in Newcastle, an establishment justly famous in its day. From school he went to study at Hamm in Germany, and from here he proceeded to Le Havre, where he took a course at the lycée. Later he entered the service of the British Consulate and became a Vice-Consul at Le Havre. He must have been an ambitious young man as he was not content with his early success but continued to study and take examinations until he became a permanent Vice-Consul, and remained in the service for forty years. He was also Lloyd's agent at Le Havre and his services were recognized when King Edward VII invested him with the Imperial Service Order. He died in 1916 during the First World War, five years before his mother.

Much rebuilding was done at The White House after the widow and her daughter made their home there with Elizabeth's sister Margaret and her brother John. John died in 1884, and Margaret followed him in 1891. It must have been a lonely life for Elizabeth and her daughter in that secluded part of Northumberland which world events passed by. Elizabeth Rowell's life spanned five reigns: George IV had been king for only a year when she was born; during her girlhood William IV was on the throne, while her marriage took place three years after Victoria's accession. There cannot have been many people who lived through the whole of the sixty glorious years, the entire reign of Victoria's son, Edward VII and part of his son's, King George V. What changes she must have seen, even in her own county of Northumberland. If only diaries and letters had been preserved to tell us what life was like at The White House at West End Town. No doubt Mrs. Rowell kept her carriage and horses, and drove out to visit her friends and relations of whom she had many scattered about South Tynedale. Daughter Annie would dutifully accompany her mother on these outings, which would at least be a break in the monotony of her drab life. On Sundays the mother and daughter would attend church at Beltingham, south of the river, and in later years at the 'new' church of All Hallows at Henshaw, which was completed in 1889. Henshaw is a hamlet which lies below Thorngrafton, close to the main Newcastle to Carlisle highway.

For eight years before her death the old lady was confined to her bed, but from the stories I have been told this did not deter her from managing her household and the affairs of her small estate. I think she must have resembled my grandfather in many ways, although I believe they were scarcely on speaking terms towards the end of Matthew Ridley's life in 1913. No doubt it was a case of Greek meeting Greek. Such was the determination of my grandfather that on the morning of his death he demanded (he never asked) to see his letters as, in his own words, he would not be there to do so at night. Mrs. Rowell was of the same calibre, and both she and her cousin became legends in their own lifetimes. They were both of the generation which prided themselves on being 'characters', and certainly in the case of Elizabeth and Matthew both succeeded. How angry Matthew would have been had he known that his cousin achieved her ambition to celebrate her hundredth birthday. Her obituary notice says rather quaintly that she took "a pardonable pride" in this achievement. An iron constitution and the care of a devoted and unselfish daughter were the chief contributions to this, had Elizabeth realized it. Annie Rowell was 76 when her mother died and only survived her by a few years. She is the epitome of the daughter who stayed at home and received little recognition for her sacrifice.

The Hexham Courant relates that "among the family treasures is a large oil-painting of the deceased lady and her two children, the figure of her husband being posthumously added from a small likeness". When Miss Annie died this picture passed into the possession of some distant Ridley relations, who in their turn left it to me. The 'treasure', which bears no signature of the artist, has a certain charm, especially in the colouring of Elizabeth's and her children's clothes. She had been a Junoesque lady, with, as one would expect from her character, a stern expression. Annie, the small girl, has a wistful look and is clutching a posy of flowers, while the future Vice-Consul, Soulsby, is arrayed in a red velvet dress under which frilly panties can be seen. Although younger than his sister he is much larger and is supported by his mother's arm, while hanging on to a gold chain suspended from her neck. The posthumous figure of Mr. Rowell was more than I could bear. He was an emaciated disembodied object floating about in space, and was only too obviously an addition by a different artist. A friend of mine obliterated the dear departed, and by doing so improved the appearance of the 'treasure'. I am sure Mrs. Rowell would not have approved, and would have regarded the obliteration as sacrilege. It is the small girl who appeals to me so strongly. Whoever the artist was he has managed to convey the impression of her sweetness of character, and the wistful, even resigned look of one who was always to take second place. For her sake I am delighted that the picture is now mine.

Few people now remember Mrs. Rowell or know anything of her life, her memory has not been preserved for posterity as has that of Mary Hollon; yet I think her story has been worth recording. The lives of these two women—the soldier's daughter who grew up in Morpeth, and the farmer's daughter from Bardon Mill—could not have been more different: Mary, who left a widower to mourn her after twenty-five years of marriage, and Elizabeth, who survived her husband by three-quarters of a century. One spent only a short part of her life in the county, the other lived in it all her long life. Mary Hollon gave and received love, and for this she is remembered; while Elizabeth Rowell commanded respect and a certain admiration for her strength of character.

When I 'get away' the picture will pass on to yet another of Elizabeth's collateral descendants, and it is for Anne that I have written this story.

12

Emily Davison, Twentieth-century Crusader

The First Blast of the Trumpet Against the Monstrous Regiment of Women.

John Knox, 1505–72

The erroneous impression still persists that Emily Wilding Davison, the militant suffragette, was born in Morpeth and that her story is associated with the town. Emily Davison never lived in the Northumbrian market town; her parents had left for London before her birth, and the house they lived in, Winton House, is now occupied by the Freemasons.

As far as Northumberland is concerned it is the village of Longhorsley which has close associations with "the wild lassie", as an old man described her to me. Emily was 21 before she first saw Northumberland and Morpeth—when she came to her father's funeral. The body had been brought from London for burial in the churchyard of St. Mary's. Almost twenty years later Emily was to join her father in the same churchyard. During her campaign for Women's Suffrage she spoke in the market-place at Morpeth, or so I have been told by one who says he remembers attending the meeting.

I have found it extremely difficult to obtain any accurate information about Emily's background. There seems to be a conspiracy among Morpethians to guard the Davison family secrets! Some people have told me that her father was a doctor, others that he was a soldier; but all my trails have petered out. Many people have volunteered to send me information which has never materialized, and I have therefore to admit defeat as far as her parents are concerned. This is most frustrating, and I am sure that when this appears in print I will be criticized and re-proached with "I could have told you". What her mother was before her marriage to Emily's father is a mystery; the stories vary from her being a housekeeper to a governess. All I can be sure of is that it was a second marriage.

It was at Longhorsely where I received really helpful information and to all those who were so forthcoming I am most grateful. The village of Longhorsley is on the A697 about four miles from Northgate on the Great North Road. To the majority of people the name Longhorsley is associated with the moors which bear its name and not with the 'long' village which borders both sides of the road. The moors, which in season are golden with gorse, are well known for their magnificent views of the Simonside range. The old rhyme has it that "When the gorse is out of bloom, Kissings out of tune." Meaning it is presumed that gorse is never out of bloom. Written off in a somewhat summary manner in most of the guide books, Longhorsley is well worth a visit, whether it be to walk through the field to St. Helen's church, which stands east of the road as the village is approached, or to look at one of the best preserved of Northumberland's many pele-towers which happily is still inhabited as a private dwelling house. There has never been a satisfactory explanation of the site of the parish church, isolated as it is from the rest of the village. Originally Norman, a complete restoration was carried out in 1783; the parish registers date from 1688.

The pele-tower, though so imposing, received no mention in the list of Border towers made in 1415. It is assumed therefore that it was probably built in the following century. Once part of the manor of Morpeth, it was owned by the Horsley family, from whom the village takes its name, subsequently passing by marriage into the ancient family of Widdrington, and again in the same manner to the Riddell family. Part of the tower was used at one time as a residence for the Roman Catholic priest, the Riddells being one of the Northumbrian families who remained loyal to the old faith. So far Longhorsley has conformed to the pattern of many Northumbrian villages, with its fortified house, or pele-tower, its rebuilt church (the Norman building possibly having been left in ruin after a border raid), and its inn, 'The Shoulder of Mutton'. Until recently 'The Rose and Thistle' was also an inn, but is now used for the display and sale of most attractive tweeds and knitwear.

Today the village is occupied with its own concerns, some of the stone-built cottages have been restored and modernized and form a pleasant courtyard off the main road. Nothing could be further removed from violence and notoriety, yet in 1913 Longhorsley was front page news. On Derby Day, 4th June, Emily Wilding Davison, one of the most extreme of the suffragettes threw herself in front of the King's horse, and died four days afterwards. For many years the militant Emily's mother kept the shop on the corner which today is known as the Corner Shop. There are people living in the village and district today who remember Mrs. Davison and her, as many people think, misguided daughter.

Emily Davison was born at Blackheath on 11th October 1872 and educated in the South—for a time at Kensington High School for Girls—before going up to Oxford. After her university career she spent several years as a governess in private families. Hearsay has it that she was for a time at Ulgham Vicarage, but this has not been authenticated. The writer has been fortunate in having met and talked to those who remember Emily Davison and, due to the kindness of a native of Longhorsley, has been lent a short biography written by G. Colmore, published by The Women's Press in 1913, when passions over the emancipation of women were still running high. From the same source as *The Life of Emily Davison* came a copy of the order of service used at a memorial service at St. George's Church, Bloomsbury, on Saturday 14th June before the coffin was brought north for burial. The following is the tribute paid on the order of service to this dedicated woman who seems to have spent the only peaceful interludes in her stormy life at Longhorsley.

IN MEMORIAM.

MISS EMILY WILDING DAVISON, B.A.

Who graduated with honours at London University, took First Class Honours in the Final Schools at Oxford University in English Language and Literature; suffered Imprisonment and endured the torture of Forcible Feeding on many occasions, and finally at Epsom offered up her Life for her Faith
on Wednesday, 4th June, 1913,
and died on Sunday, 8th June, 1913.
Greater Love hath no man than this, that he
lay down his life for his Friend.

In the terms of history (fifty-seven years) it is only a short time

Alexander Ridley

The writer's father,
Robert Ridley

The writer as a child

since her death, and yet already she had become a legend. It is difficult, apart from her work for the Suffragette Movement—which can be read in the history of the times—to build up a true picture of Emily's life and background. Before the death of her father the family seems to have been in comfortable circumstances, belonging to what then would be called upper-middle-class. The family fortunes took a turn for the worse when Mrs. Davison became a widow, as she baked bread (not very good say the local people!) and sold it, among other things, in the shop at Longhorsley. The following letter from Emily expresses concern about money matters.

> Today we have been very busy, and I have been out with Mama. She has decided that I am to return to College [Holloway College] tomorrow. It is very hard to leave them all . . . but what can one do? Mama has to pay £20 a term for me, and it must not be wasted. I do not know if I can stay on after this term, as we do not know how matters are yet, so I must make the best of this term. . . .

It was to Longhorsley that Emily came to find refuge after her prison sentences. Many of her fellow suffragettes disapproved strongly of her violence, and were of the opinion that by her militant behaviour she was doing more harm than good to their cause. Certainly it seems rather extreme to horse-whip an unoffending Presbyterian Minister in Aberdeen because she mistook him for Lloyd-George! Throwing stones at the then Sir Walter Runciman did nothing either to endear her to law-abiding people. Yet believe in the cause she must, or how could she have endured the forcible feeding, having hose-pipes turned on her, and survived the injuries she sustained when she threw herself down the iron staircase in Holloway?

Although Longhorsley was her refuge, she herself said that she had no love for the country. In some very bad poetry she expressed her feelings: "Oh, London! How I feel thy magic spell," and several lines which the reader shall be spared until her finale,

> The centre of the universe is here!
> This is the hub, the very fount of life.

Her physical appearance, so it is said, was attractive; she was very feminine, a churchwoman, spoke very quickly, and had a habit of holding her head to one side. She loved walking in the

10

lanes round Longhorsley and picking wild raspberries, a far cry
from hunger-striking in Manchester and London prisons. During
her active campaign she sometimes used disguises, wearing a
switch of dark hair (her own was fair). Could there be any connection between the bottle of lady's hair dye found hidden in a
chimney in the house at Longhorsley and the 'dark switch'? It
is impossible to understand the workings of her mind, especially
by one who has never had to fight for her rights. It is easy to have
hindsight and to pass judgement on others when one has not
been in the same position. Yet it is difficult to condone her final
desperate act. How could a woman who believed in God throw
away her life and, what is even harder to understand, endanger
the lives of men and horses.

That she planned the whole affair there is no doubt. She even
sewed the colours of the suffragettes inside her jacket before she
set off for Epsom. George V was there to see his horse Anmer
run in what was to be the most dramatic Derby in the long history
of the race. The horses were bunched together as they were
approaching Tattenham Corner when a woman dashed under the
rails and seized the bridle of the King's horse, bringing down
Anmer and his jockey Herbert Jones, who was badly injured.
The race went on as the unknown woman lay still and quiet on
the course, but the winner Craiganour was disqualified and the
race awarded to Aboyeur. Thus ended Emily Davison's Derby
Day and, four days afterwards, her life. Her mother far away in
Northumberland told friends that at the precise time Emily
made her mad dash towards the horses a bird flew through the
little house on the corner, although all the doors and windows
were shut.

It has always been assumed that it was the King's horse that
actually struck Emily as she lay on the Derby Course; but, when
searching through old copies of *The Morpeth Herald*, I read an
account of the inquest, which stated that two police officers who
gave evidence said it was impossible to identify the exact horse
in the general mêlée. This is a typical example of dramatization; it
is a much better story to say that she was killed by the King's
horse. (Herbert Jones, who was riding the royal entry, was convinced that his horse was responsible, and this preyed on his mind
to such an extent that years later he committed suicide.) The evidence of identification was given by Emily's half-brother, who is

described as an officer in the Royal Navy. This makes one suspect that what money there was had gone to the first Davison family, as in 1913 officers in the Royal Navy were expected to have private means.

The body of Emily was brought by train to Newcastle and thence to Morpeth, where the funeral took place on Sunday 15th June, amid scenes which strangely resembled a miner's gala. Crowds gathered on the steep slopes which rise from the road sides on the way from Morpeth Railway station to the 'High Church'; one cynic who was there assured me that it was as a spectator not a mourner that he attended the funeral. The Benwell Silver Band played lustily, and eight little girls dressed in white carried madonna lilies. The suffragettes attended *en masse*, wearing their green, white and violet colours to symbolize 'Give Women Votes'. One strange floral tribute was a bunch of pinks in the form of a sun bonnet bearing this peculiar inscription: "From a gambler's wife. Convict no more, nor shame, nor dole, Depart-A God-Enfranchized Soul." Emily's funeral was as dramatic as the last desperate act of her life. It seems it was only the more fanatical in the fight for the rights of women who truly mourned poor Emily Davison; the more level-headed felt she had done the cause more harm than good and had antagonized many former sympathizers.

Emily Davison was one of those unfortunate people who cannot realize that violence only begets violence. Her life seems to have brought her little happiness, and most of the expressions of sympathy which were made at the time were qualified. One of her ardent admirers is worth quoting, as this makes clear the way extremists think: "With her clear and unflinching vision, she realized that now, as in days of old, to awake the conscience of the people, a human life would be needed as a sacrifice ... she heard the call and made the answer 'I come'." Of such stuff are martyrs made, yet she is no heroine to those who remember her. The more tolerant hope 'The wild lassie' has found peace at last.

13

Foray into Cumberland

Wi' a hundred pipers an' a', an' a',
Wi' a hundred pipers an' a', an' a',
We'll up an' gie them a blaw, a blaw,
Wi' a hundred pipers an' a', an' a',
Oh! its owre the border, awa', awa',
Its owre the border awa', awa',
We'll on an' we'll march to Carlisle ha',
Wi' its yetts, and castles an' a', an' a'.

Words by Lady Nairne
From the Morven Collection of Scottish Songs

It seems appropriate that as Cumberland was the county to which my great-great-grandfather Thomas Ridley ventured with his bride, Cumberland was the writer's first foray beyond the borders of her native county. Lipwood Well, where I was born, stands midway between the cities of Newcastle upon Tyne and Carlisle, and some twelve miles or so from the Cumberland-Northumberland border. At one time there was a milestone a little way east of Lipwood Well, which gave the distances, "Newcastle 28½ miles, Carlisle 28½'. The milestone stood at the brow of a hill locally known as Topping's Bank, commemorating by its name an old man who lived in one of the nearby cottages at Willow Gap.

Although no county in the British Isles can ever compare with Northumberland, at least in the opinion of a Ridley, North Cumberland is extremely beautiful and virtually unspoilt. When the visitor approaches the Cumberland border by way of Halt-whistle and Greenhead and has recovered from the shock of the giant tower-like structures which dominate the waste that is Spadeadam, then North Cumberland unfolds as rich agricultural land in the valleys, while the moorland rolls north towards the Scottish border.

Where the raiders once took refuge on Spadeadam waste is a rocket-testing station, and the towers house the rockets. From the security point of view the position is almost impregnable as there is only one major road. From the aesthetic point of view it is less pleasing and reminds one forcibly of the horrors of modern warfare. The coming of the rocket station brought hundreds of new workers into the district from all over the country. Many of those employed at Spadeadam live in or near the market-town of Brampton, and reports have it that these newcomers have integrated remarkably well with the local inhabitants.

The most attractive road into North Cumberland is the secondary one which leaves the A.69 at Greenhead. The writer's own name for this is the 'back' road. In my childhood days the ascent of Greenhead Bank on the A.69 was considered so dangerous that nervous occupants of cars walked, leaving the driver to climb the hill, crunching away in bottom gear, while the passengers rejoined the car if it ever reached the top. It is only recently that improvements have been carried out, as so many of the heavy lorries have lost control when descending from the west. The 'back' road leads to Gilsland, a village which is partly in each county. Administered by Cumberland though it is, the dividing line is in the middle of the village. In fact, a short time ago when speaking to the members of the Gilsland Women's Institute (which is in the Cumberland Federation), the Chairman assured me that I was standing on Northumbrian soil.

The railway journey from Haydon Bridge to Carlisle is full of variety. After leaving the Valley of the South Tyne at Haltwhistle, and passing through some wild and dramatic scenery, the Eden Valley is crossed at Wetheral. As a child, for some reason I regarded it as a great achievement to recite the names of the railway stations from memory. Bardon Mill, Haltwhistle, Greenhead, Gilsland, Low Row, Brampton Junction, Wetheral, Heads Nook, Scotby and Carlisle.

Now, with the exception of Bardon Mill, which won the battle against its closure, the only stations still open are Brampton and Haltwhistle.

I have in my possession a guide, published by Ward, Lock & Co in 1899, entitled *Hexham, Gilsland and the Borderland*. Taking no chances, Messrs. Ward, Lock & Co. warn the readers that

Every care has been taken in the compilation of this volume to render it accurate and trustworthy. But it is the lot of all human beings—even editors of Guide Books who, of all men, should be most careful—to err. In this busy age, too, changes take place, both in town and country, with marvellous rapidity, and thwart at times the efforts of the most painstaking writer.

If the writers of 1899 found "changes taking place with marvellous rapidity", then there is even less hope for a writer in 1970.

This is not a guide to North Cumberland, but the reminiscences of one who as a child was taken on many happy outings in this Border Country. I imagine my interest in this part of Cumberland was fostered by the many Cumberland men who were in my father's employment, especially one whom I remember with love and affection. His name was Jack Watson, and he always pronounced Carlisle as Carel. The speech of the two counties is completely different, varying, of course, in different parts of Cumberland as it does in Northumberland. There are differences too in the people themselves—the man from North Cumberland has less in common with Scotland than the Northumbrian. The land border between Cumberland and Scotland is short; is it because the Solway penetrates so deeply and curtails communication? Cumberland was part of the Western March in the days of the Border Raiding, and one of the most famous Wardens was a Howard of Naworth whose sobriquet was 'Belted Will'. Naworth is one of the great Border fortresses, and is to Cumberland what Alnwick Castle is to Northumberland.

It was in the fourteenth century that licence to crenellate Naworth was granted by Edward III to Ralph Dacre, whose family remained prominent in Cumberland until the failure of the male line, when the Dacre heiress married the colourful character 'Belted Will'. Although this best known of the Howards has been so much associated with Naworth, it was at Greystoke Castle that he died. This marriage between a Dacre and a Howard was remarkable for the fact that they were half brother and sister. To keep money in the family led to many peculiar strategies, which very often the church conveniently arranged. Naworth has seen many changes since 1335, and in the last century a disastrous fire destroyed most of the building, only Lord William Howard's tower remaining. The castle was restored by the sixth Earl of

Carlisle, who employed the celebrated architect Salvin, who was responsible for the Morpeth Tower. The heir to the earldom of Carlisle bears the title of Lord Morpeth; the family at one time having close connections with the Northumbrian town on the Wansbeck.

The setting of the castle is particularly attractive, set as it is in well-wooded parkland, and approached by a long drive from the A.69. At certain times the castle is open to the public, and many are the treasures to be seen. Rosalind, Countess of Carlisle, who died in the early part of this century, was an ardent temperance reformer. So bigoted was this extraordinary woman that she is reputed to have poured brandy into the lake at Castle Howard, the Carlisle's famous Vanbrugh house in Yorkshire.

At one time there were no public houses on any of the Cumberland estates of the Earls of Carlisle. There is a 'Howard Arms' in Brampton, of which no doubt the pioneering Rosalind would have disapproved strongly; a view which would not be shared by 'Belted Will'.

The farmhouses are different from those in Northumberland, most of them being built of red sandstone, while the soil in many parts is a rich red colour. Once the Cumberland border is crossed at Gilsland, the burns of Northumberland become becks and ghylls. The River Irthing which waters this part of the county is at its most beautiful south of Birdoswald Camp.

Here the red sandstone cliffs rise steeply from the river banks and are crowned with trees, which overlook the Irthing as it makes a gigantic curve.

North Cumberland has this in common with its neighbouring county—that apart from the great Roman station of Birdoswald near Gilsland, it is largely neglected by the tourist. Possibly this accounts for its charm. To me at least the north of Cumberland is more genuine—and, of course, much less sophisticated—than the world-famous Lake District. Magnificent though the English Lake District is, it has since the last war become so commercialized that for me at least it has lost its attraction. With the opening of the new motorway it is even more accessible for people from the great cities of Lancashire. The Lake District too, lacks the history of the Eden and Irthing valleys, and of course Prince Charlie was never there! No doubt someone who reads this will have some local story of a visit from the Young Chevalier, but the places visited by Charlie rival in number Queen Elizabeth I's beds and the churches where Cromwell stabled his horses.

My first visit to Carlisle was with my father, when I was so small that I can remember being carried in his arms into the 'Crown and Mitre Hotel'. It was there in 'The Crown and Mitre' that I saw for the first time a picture of young Charlie and his unhappy ancestress Mary Queen of Scots. Last year I went into a vastly changed hotel but the pictures which fired my enthusiasm long ago are still there. When I was a child all the famous people in history whom I heard about were either saints or villains; now having grown older I have learnt that people are neither. There are no blacks and whites, only greys. Although I still picture a romantic young prince riding into Carlisle at the head of his army, I realize now how tragic was the episode known the world over as the '45. Here I am concerned only with the time Charles Edward Stuart spent in Cumberland. Out of the six weeks he was in England, three of those were spent in and near the market town of Brampton. It was on 8th November 1745 that the Jacobite Army crossed the Border Esk at The Riddings, not far from where Sir Walter Scott's Young Lochinvar swam the same river to rescue his bride from Netherby. It is amazing how many connections there are with Cumberland and the ill-fated House of Stuart. When the great-grandfather of the Young Chevalier stepped out of a window in Whitehall to meet his death on the scaffold, a Graham of Netherby stood beside him. The Bible which Charles I gave to Graham is now at Netherby, where Sir Fergus Graham, a former member of Parliament for Darlington and ex-High Sheriff of Cumberland lives. The writer has had the privilege of holding this Bible in her hands.

Mary Queen of Scots' first English prison was Carlisle Castle. Did her great-great-great-grandson think of her tragedy as he stepped on English soil; did it make him more than ever determined to restore his father, the ageing, morose Old Chevalier, to the throne of Great Britain? Cumberland held few happy memories for the Stuarts; it was on that desolate land close to the Border, Solway Moss, that the father of Mary Queen of Scots was defeated by an English army. It is said that James V 'The Poor Man's King', died of a broken heart a few days after the defeat. The dying man reached Falkland Palace when he heard the news that his Queen Mary of Guise had given birth to a daughter and he uttered a prophecy which for once came true. The King's words were: "It cam' wi a lass, it'll gan' wi' a lass". Marjorie, the daughter of the great Bruce, married the Lord High Steward of Scotland, who founded the House of Stuart; and the last of the line to rule was Anne, the half sister of the Old Chevalier, or the Old Pretender as his enemies called him.

Yet perhaps the three weeks 'Bonnie Charlie' was in Cumberland were the happiest he ever spent. The victory of Preston Pans was behind him, Johnny Cope had ridden to Berwick with the news of his own defeat, and the Jacobite army was over the Border. It was in Brampton that the Stuart Prince made his headquarters. The house where he stayed has been preserved and is distinguished by the words 'Prince Charles House' in bold lettering. Quite recently the house where his staff was quartered was demolished. The Duke of Perth besieged Carlisle, which very soon capitulated, and to Brampton came the mayor to hand over the keys of Carlisle. There is still in existence a record of the household book kept by the Duke of Perth while the army was at Brampton. It is an interesting fact that there is no evidence of looting and that all accounts were paid.

On Tuesday 12th November, 4½ stones of 'bife' were bought for 2d. a pound, one sheep cost 6s., ten 'poulets' 3s. 6d., two geese 2s. 2d., five ducks 3s. 4d. Brandy was 21s. an anker, which was equivalent to 10 gallons. On the 14th, when the Prince dined at Squire Warwick's house 77½ pounds of butter are entered in the records at 4d. a pound, and numerous ducks, hens and 'poulets'. In Tullie House, Carlisle's Museum, is a winged chair from 'Squire' Warwick's house in which Prince Charlie sat. None of the original upholstery remains, souvenir hunters have done their worst. Life must have felt good for Charlie as he rode into Carlisle, drums beating and pipes playing. Along English Street rode and marched the Jacobite army to proclaim at the Market Cross, King James III and VIII by the Grace of God. The Market Cross still stands in front of the old town hall, which to the credit of Carlisle is to be preserved, although a modern civic centre is now the headquarters of the city council. As you walk along English Street today towards the old town hall look above the very modern frontage of Marks and Spencers. There are two inscribed stones, the first says "Prince Charles Edward Stuart stayed here 1745" and on the second, "The Duke of Cumberland stayed here 1746." The original house in which these distant cousins stayed was demolished to make way for Marks and Spencers. Even more incongruous is that when Charlie was marching south to Derby he stayed in Kendal, in what is now the Y.W.C.A. Hardly a suitable lodging for a Stuart. Cumberland has always been unfortunate in the royal dukes who have taken their title from the county, but none has been more loathed than William Augustus rightly named 'The Butcher'.

This is not the place to discuss what happened after Culloden, but the atrocities carried out by the orders of the Hanoverians are a blot on English history. The only mitigation is that the man behind the carnage was a German of the very worst type.

This was all in the future when Prince Charlie led his army out of Carlisle towards Penrith on the march towards London and a glorious restoration. He was still the dashing young man in the tartan marching with his men. The following rather inferior verse is worth quoting if only to give some idea of the feelings he roused in the ordinary people.

> Over the lonely moors we ride,
> Booted and spurred with sword at side,
> Our hearts beating true with loyal pride,
> And we're off to fight for Prince Charlie.
>
> Fearing no foe, onward we go,
> What Cumberland lads can do we will show;
> And Cumberland arms can strike a hard blow,
> And we're off to fight for Prince Charlie.
>
> Gaily we sing, let the hills ring,
> Riding o'er heather and bracken and ling,
> Riding to fight for our lawful king,
> Riding to fight for Prince Charlie.
>
> Women may sigh, battle is nigh,
> Beat us they may, but still we can try,
> And we'll show them how Cumberland lads can die,
> Fighting for Bonnie Prince Charlie.

Death was to be the fate of many who marched for the south on that winter day, death on the gallows for some in their own city of Carlisle. In Penrith the Prince spent the night in 'The George Hotel', then left for the long climb over Shap. He would not see

Cumberland again until Derby was a bitter memory. On 6th December, another 'Black Friday'—just as 9th September when James IV fell at Flodden was known for hundreds of years—the army began its terrible retreat from Derby.

The writer has no intention of going over the rights and wrongs of the decision to turn for the north. Many historians think that had the Prince not been over-ruled by his advisers, he could have taken London and restored the Stuart monarchy. Whether this would have been a good thing or not is a question which can never be answered now. Only the facts of the retreat and its aftermath are incontrovertible.

It was on Thursday 19th December, about nine in the morning, that a tired disheartened army once more entered the city they had left with such high hopes. One of the many of the terrible mistakes which form part of the pattern of the '45 was to leave a garrison in Carlisle Castle.

Four hundred men were left behind; two companies of The Duke of Perth's Regiment (the Duke himself was to die as he was carried on board the French ship in which Prince Charlie left Scotland forever in September of 1746) a company of Ogilvy's, Glen Buckets and Roy Stuarts, and many of the wounded men. Colonel John Hamilton was appointed Governor of the Castle and Francis Townley from Burnley in Lancashire in command of the town. (Some years ago when the writer was speaking in Burnley she was taken to see the house in which this brave man lived and which is now the property of Burnley Town Council.)

On the next day, 20th December, Prince Charlie marched out of Carlisle for the last time, making for the Border Esk.

> The Esk was swollen, sae red and sae deep,
> But shouther to shouther the brave lads keep.

The lads kept shouther to shouther to dam the swollen river and allow the cavalry to cross to the Scottish side.

After Prince Charlie abandoned Carlisle the Hanoverian retributions began. There were so many prisoners they could not all be accommodated in the castle dungeons, and many were incarcerated in Carlisle Cathedral. If you lift up the cushions in the choir stalls, carved on the wood can be seen initials which are said to have been done by Jacobite prisoners. Many brave men, Englishmen and Scotsmen, met their deaths by hanging on

Harraby Hill, while others died of starvation in the castle dungeons. 'The Licking Stones' are pointed out today by the guides; no water was given to these wretched men, and there was, of course, no light. The story of the '45 as far as Cumberland and Carlisle were concerned was over, but memories linger on.

At Cumwhitton which is 9 miles east of Carlisle, the School house was known as 'The Piper's Stile', so called, it is said, because an exhausted Highlander dropped out on the retreat, was befriended by the local people and spent the rest of his life in their midst, playing for them at 'The Piper's Stile'. There is an excellent book *Prince Charlie And The Borderland* by David Johnstone Beattie published by Charles Thurnam & Sons of Carlisle in 1928. As Ward, Lock's guide was so anxious to emphasize, changes take place with "marvellous rapidity", and owners of Jacobite relics in Cumberland may have parted with them years ago. Certainly many changes have taken place since Thomas Ridley took his bride to 'Ye Banks', and many have taken place since my father carried me into 'The Crown and Mitre'. Let me make this quite clear—I have never been carried out of 'The Crown and Mitre'!

One place that has not changed much through the years is Lanercost's beautiful priory church. The setting is so wonderful, and the church has an atmosphere of peace and tranquillity. It was somewhere about the year 1166 that the foundations were laid for this monastic house, where eventually an Order of Augustinian Canons was established. There near the River Irthing these canons lived in comparative peace for about 370 years until that destroyer of religious houses, Henry VIII, set about his infamous dissolution. Comparative peace is rather an understatement for anyone living near the Border, and Lanercost suffered visitations from the Scots on many occasions. A local poet wrote:

> Corbrigge is a toun, thei brent it whan thei cam;
> Tou hous of religioun, Laynercoste and Hexham,
> Thei chaced the chanons out, their goodes bare away.
> And robbed all about; the bestis to prey.

Many and varied were the 'visitors' who came to Lanercost. Edward I on his way to and from hammering the Scots was a frequent caller, on one occasion bringing his Queen Eleanor with him. William Wallace came and left a trail of ruin behind him, which the canons in time restored; then in his turn came the Bruce and meted out the same treatment; and, not to be outdone, David II emulated Wallace and Bruce. Richly endowed though the order had been, much of the land had to be sold to repair the damage done by the Scotsmen.

This pillaging and destruction was not a Scottish prerogative; the Cumberland men used the same methods when they made retaliatory raids over the Border. It was a way of life which again is portrayed in typical Border verse.

"A Reiver's Song"

Over the borderland wha will gang with me?
Saddle your horses and buckle your blades,
We will bring back with us fat Scottish cattle,
Good Scottish horses and fair Scottish maids.
Gretna's behind us, all Scotland before us,
Nae halt till full fifty fat roebuck we've slain,
An' our purses well filled full O' bright Scottish monies,
And then we'll make southward for Naworth again.

Back o'er the borderland, back o'er the moors,
Sweethearts await us wi' kiss and wi' smile,
Driving the cattle and horses we've captured,
Driving them back again, back to Carlisle.

After the Dissolution a branch of the Dacre family became the owners of Lanercost and remained so until 1716. The senior branch of the family were at the nearby castle of Naworth, but, as with so many of these old families, the last of the line was a girl, an heiress who married in 1577 the Warden of The Marches, 'Belted Will'. It was the great-grandson of this marriage who became the first Earl of Carlisle in 1661.

Lanercost too saw changes of ownership, as after 1716 it became Crown property until bought by the Earl of Carlisle in 1869. Lady Cecilia Roberts, who before her marriage was a Howard, transferred the ownership to the Ministry of Works, who maintain it today.

As is to be expected there are in the church many tombs of Dacres and Howards; one is of a Dacre who fought at Flodden. There is a touching memorial to the wife of one of the Howards who died in childbirth.

> Twenty years a maiden,
> One year a wife,
> One hour a mother,
> And then departed life.

My memory may have failed me as to the exact wording of this pathetic little verse, which presumably refers to Mary Howard, born Parke, who died three days after she had given birth to a son who became the ninth Earl of Carlisle.

There is an excellent Guide to Lanercost written by John R. H. Moorman, M.A., D.D. How much more flowery in their language were the guidebooks of the last century, and Ward, Lock & Co's publication of 1899 is no exception. There are several pages devoted to the attractions of Gilsland, and instructions to the visitor on what to wear, what to do and where to stay. The railways then were in their heyday, and we are told how the whole of the district can be covered by that means of transport. Rather an exaggeration even for those days—I have never heard of a railway service to Bewcastle. But go to Bewcastle by some means to see one of the only two early Christian Crosses in Cumberland, the other being at Gosforth in the extreme south-east of the county.

Bewcastle lies in wild fell country, and on a road that leads on to the Scottish Border. The cross which stands in the churchyard is Anglian, probably dating from the eighth century. There is so much controversy about the meaning of the symbols and inscriptions that I have no intention of becoming involved!

This part of North Cumberland is associated with Sir Walter Scott, as it was at Gilsland that he set the scene of *Guy Mannering*, basing it on the legend of a notorious inn, 'Mump's Ha', and making his chief female character Meg Merrilies. To quote:

In the church of Over or Upper Denton are the tombstones of the family of 'Meg', she herself it is believed, lying under the stone inscribed: Mump's Hall. Here lieth the body of Margarett Carrick, ye wife of Tho. Carrick, who departed this life ye 4 of Decem 1717 in the 100 year of her age.

Gilsland was also famous as a 'watering place'. The Spa Hotel and Hydro, the famous Shaws Hotel, of years gone by is described in the guide as "one of the most comfortable homes from home in the district, and has recently been refurnished and completely transformed. The hotel is close to the famous mineral springs of the district; and intimately connected with Sir Walter Scott, who laid some of the scenes of his novels here. An omnibus from the hotel meets the trains at the station." Terms. Pension 52s. 6d. to 73s. 6d. Saturday to Monday 15s. I must hastily add this was in 1899, not 1970.

If you were really in the money you could have a week at 'The Crown and Mitre' for 63s. Since those halcyon days The Shaws Hotel has been a convalescent home among other things, but I doubt if it will ever again offer the facilities it did in Queen Victoria's golden days.

I realize how inadequate this chapter on North Cumberland is; there are so many places and episodes I could have mentioned, but I have stuck to events and places which fired my imagination when a child and the stories of which I have tried to trace to their logical conclusions.

A few years ago I spent three weeks in Cumberland on what is called a Group Tour of Women's Institutes. To the uninitiated this means that in spring and autumn so many institutes within a group, usually named after some well-known part of the county, hold a series of meetings and 'outside' speakers are brought in. I travelled the length and breadth of the county: from industrial West Cumberland to Ravenglass and Gosforth, to Longtown on the Border (the day I went to Netherby and saw Charles I's Bible) to Weatheral, and the Lake district and into the John Peel country. It was an experience I enjoyed enormously, particularly one most lovely evening when the meeting was held near Ullswater at Watermillock. (It was out of the season and Lakeland had returned to normality.)

My most outstanding memory is of walking by the Solway at Skinburness when the sun was setting. The rays of light formed a path across the water that made it appear one could walk across to the Scottish side where Criffel was merging into the dimness of the twilight.

There is something so soothing about the air of the Solway that it is not surprising that when the late King George V was recovering from his serious illness in 1928 Skinburness was seriously considered for his convalescence. But the size of his entourage was such that Skinburness could not accommodate him and the King went to Eastbourne instead.

It seemed a long time since a small girl of Lipwood Well was out walking with her father and a beloved dog whose name was Moss. My home was close to the main Newcastle–Carlisle railway, and poor Moss was killed by a train. My understanding father picked me up in his arms and rushed home with me, telling me that Moss had decided to go and live in Carlisle, and that my father had actually seen Moss jump into a first-class compartment and start to read *The Times*. It was many years before I discovered the truth. Sometimes when the Irish Mail went past, the 'Paddy'—as it was and still is called—used to wake me up, and I lay wondering what Moss was doing.

So my interest in Cumberland and Bonnie Prince Charlie started through a horse and a dog. How many memories have been evoked as I have written this chapter, but by praising another county I have in no way been unfaithful to my own; perhaps it has made me love it even more.

14

The Scottish Side of the Border

Should auld aquaintance be forgot,
And never brought to min'?
Should auld acquaintance be forgot,
And auld lang syne.

Burns

As Northumberland marches with the Scottish Border, it is not
surprising that my first visit to a 'foreign' country was to Scotland.
The Scottish Border counties, in common with Northumberland,
are largely neglected by the tourists, who rush north to Edinburgh,
and the country that lies beyond the Forth. The tourists thus miss
some of the most wonderful scenery in the British Isles (second
only to Northumberland in the writer's estimation). Within the
boundaries of Roxburghshire and Berwickshire the historic
monuments equal the scenery in their diversity and interest.
Ruined abbeys, castles and great houses abound; and the first-
named county is associated with Scotland's famous poet and
writer, Sir Walter Scott.

I remember vividly the first time I crossed the Border by that
most dramatic of crossings, the Carter Bar. I was a very small
girl, and I know I had no sleep the night before because I was
going to Scotland. We made a very early start as my father was
going to the Ram Sales at Kelso, which are always held on the
second Friday in September. My home was then at Lipwood Well,
near Haydon Bridge, so our road to Kelso led us by way of
North Tyne to Watling Street, and thence by Woodburn to where
the A68 joins the road from Otterburn at Elishaw Bridge. The
road to the Border then climbs from Catcleugh Reservoir to the
Carter, where the signposts England-and-Scotland stand on the
frontier. I can still remember the thrill when the car stopped and
climbing out I stood with a foot in both countries. I have crossed

the Border many times since that long ago morning both by way of the Carter and by the many roads which link Scotland with Northumberland and Cumberland, yet I have never lost the thrill of 'Crossing the Border'.

A short time ago I took part in a television programme called "Home Ground", a great deal of which was shot in the wild Cheviot country of the Carter Bar. I lost count of the number of times I ran from Scotland into England and back again, as I declaimed the bloody history of this frontier.

Here on the Carter Bar was fought the last great Border fray, the Raid of the Redeswire, in 1575, an event still commemorated by the 'Jethart' (Jedburgh) Callants, as the young men of Jedburgh are called. Every July the Callants gallop up to the summit of the Carter, as part of the custom of their Common Riding. These Common Ridings are held in most of the Border towns. Hawick and Jedburgh have their Cornet and Callants; Galashiels its 'Braw Lad'; and Selkirk its 'Souter' (shoemaker). Only one 'souter' returned from the field of Flodden, and the story is that the Selkirk folk felt they had been deserted on that fatal field by the Earl of Home. An old rhyme runs;

> Up with the Souters of Selkirk
> And down with the Earl of Home.

This rhyme was recalled when the freedom of Selkirk was conferred upon Sir Alec Douglas-Home when he was Prime Minister.

The road from the Carter descends by many twists and turns to the town of Jedburgh, dominated by the ruins of its once-magnificient abbey. The town stands on the Jed Water, in the heart of what was once Jed Forest. It is a typical Scottish Border town of sturdy stone-built houses and narrow streets. Jedburgh's pride is its abbey, which was founded in 1118 by King David I. Standing so close to the Border, Jedburgh suffered grievously from the incessant warfare which raged for centuries between the two countries. Between 1300 and 1545 the abbey was destroyed seven times, the last occasion being when the Earl of Hertford laid waste to the Border. Jedburgh was the first Border abbey I ever saw and I am sure I was greatly impressed, but, being then a very small girl, I must admit that I had more interest in 'Jedburgh snails', which are a sweet peculiar to the town. What 'cockles' are to Berwick upon Tweed so 'snails' are to Jedburgh.

Many years after my first visit to the town on the Jed Water I discovered that Mary, Queen of Scots had stayed in what is called Queen Mary's House. The ill-fated Queen of Scots had come to visit the assizes, or that was the official reason given. Now that I have learnt more of the story of this queen who allowed her heart to rule her head, it seems more likely she had come to be near James Hepburn, Earl of Bothwell. It was for this Border raider's sake that Mary eventually lost her crown. It was while she was staying in this bastle-house that Mary heard that Bothwell had been injured in a skirmish in his native valley of Liddesdale and was nursing his wounds in his castle of Hermitage. This grim stronghold, now the property of the Ministry of Works, stands on the 'water' which bears its name. Of all the castles I have ever visited, Hermitage has the most eerie and sinister atmosphere. Now roofless, it is a huge square pile of grim character. Legend has it that so much evil has been done at Hermitage that eventually it will sink. Certainly the history associated with James Hepburn's refuge is some of the most blood-thirsty on the Border, even in Liddesdale, which was notorious for its wild inhabitants until long ago after the union of the Crowns. The oldest part of Hermitage dates from the thirteenth century and was built by William de Soulis. For conspiring against The Bruce, Soulis forfeited his castle on the Hermitage Water, and it became the property of the Border family of Graham; passing from them by marriage to a branch of the notorious Douglases.

One of the gruesome legends is that a prisoner of the Douglases, Sir Alexander Ramsay, was starved to death within its walls, though—if one can believe the story—the wretched man managed to survive for seventeen long years on grains of corn which fell from the granary above his cell. In 1492 the Douglases left Liddesdale for Bothwell Castle on the Clyde and the Earls of Bothwell became the owners of Hermitage. As its name implies, the site of this sinister building was originally a hermitage, although little is known about its history.

It was in 1566 that the Queen of Scots rode from Jedburgh to Hermitage to visit her Border raider. This ride has become famous, not only for the fact that a Queen undertook this long and tiring ride to visit one of her subjects, but that as a result of the undertaking the Queen developed an illness from which it took her weeks to recover. The cramped litttle room in the Queen's House where the Queen lay in her bed is still shown to visitors. It might have been better for Mary Stuart had she died in that little room, than to live as she did, a prisoner of Elizabeth of England for nineteen years, until that rival Queen signed Mary's death-warrant. It was by her manner of dying, not by living, that Mary of Scotland achieved immortality. What happened during that visit to Bothwell will never be known. Her friends affirmed that it was merely the act of a sympathetic woman to one of the few men who had, in his way, given her loyal support. Her enemies—and the Scottish Queen had many—said that Bothwell was already her lover. This unhappy woman was one of those people who in life and death have roused bitter controversy; she is either adored or vilified. Mary Stuart's epitome should be the words she embroidered as a girl: "My beginning is in my end." Whatever the motives for her visit to that desolate outpost of her kingdom, Mary was to suffer dearly. Not only did she suffer physically from the exposure of her long ride over the moss, but her reputation was to be even more blackened by her enemies.

In the museum which has been established in Queen Mary's house is a little French watch which is thought to be the one she lost on her return journey from Hermitage. It was discovered in the moss between Hermitage and Jedburgh centuries after Mary's death. What strikes the twentieth-century visitor to the Queen's House so forcibly is the inadequate accommodation and the lack of comfort. It comes as no surprise to read that the Four Marys huddled together in one bed in an effort to keep warm! In that eventful year in the life of the Queen of Scots, the great abbey of Jedburgh was already a ruin, a ruin which like the memory of the unhappy Queen survives after four hundred years. It was in another of Scotland's ruined abbeys that Mary spent her last night in her own country—the lovely abbey of Dundrennan close to the Solway in Kirkcudbrightshire.

This part of Mary's history was unknown to the child of long ago when she first saw Jedburgh. I knew that the Scottish queen had been executed by her cousin of England, and I had gazed at pictures of Mary and Elizabeth in a rather lurid history book which had been my grandfather's. To my childish mind, one was a good queen who died on the block, and one was a bad

queen who wore a red wig. I can remember dressing up as Mary
and wearing a rather scratchy pie-frill round my neck as an
improvised ruffle. I staged Mary's last moments on many occasions
but always managed to rise from the dead without any marks of
my ordeal.

Although I can remember so clearly seeing Jedburgh for the
first time I have only the haziest recollection of the road from
Jedburgh to Kelso. I am always filled with admiration for those
writers who can recall with such exactitude and wealth of detail
their childhood's experiences. I must admit my memories are
patchy; some events are as clear as though they had happened
yesterday, while others are blurred and indistinct. Perhaps my
father was in a hurry to get to the ram sales and tired of answering
my incessant barrage of questions. Although my grandfather's
flock of pedigree Border Leicester sheep had been dispersed after
his death, my father still maintained his interest in the breed and
made what can only be described as an annual pilgrimage to
Kelso. This was the first time I had been taken, and I was filled
with self-importance. I can truthfully say that I remember every
minute of my first visit to Kelso, which is without doubt the
loveliest town on Tweedside.

Kelso is unlike any other Border town. It is more reminiscent of
France with its square which resembles a French *place*. Sir Walter
Scott described Kelso as "the most beautiful if not the most
romantic town in Scotland".

The Tweed is spanned by an early nineteenth-century bridge
by John Rennie who also designed Waterloo, Southwark and
London bridges. The bridge at Kelso was completed in 1803. The
Tweed rises in the wild uplands of Peebleshire at Tweedsmuir—
from which John Buchan took his title of Lord Tweedsmuir—
and enters the North Sea at Berwick. In its course, partly as a
boundary between England and Scotland, it flows through varied
and magnificent scenery.

As the traveller to Kelso crosses Rennie's bridge, he is confronted by the ruins of the abbey, which suffered so greatly in
the time of Henry VIII. The same King David who founded the
abbey at Jedburgh was also the founder of Kelso, whose first
occupants were monks from Picardy. This may have had some
influence on the French atmosphere of the town. A Stewart king,
James III of Scotland was crowned in Kelso Abbey. At the

height of its prosperity it was one of the richest and most important abbeys on the Scottish side of the Border, until its story became the all-too-familiar one of devastation by fire and sword. The monks of Kelso made their last stand against the Earl of Hertford, a man whose memory is still hated by Borderers. It was in 1545 that Hertford overcame the garrison, and it and the monks were massacred. After the Dissolution of the Monastries Kelso became the property of the Ker family, ancestors of the Innes-Kers, who are Dukes of Roxburghe. Floors Castle, the ducal home, overlooks Tweed, and resembles a French château in its elaborate architecture. The original spelling was Fleurs, and one is again reminded of France.

The Dower House of the Roxburghes is now a hotel, 'Ednam House', and in recent years I have on two occasions spoken there to the members of Kelso Tea Club. A far cry from the day when an excited little girl saw this Tweedside town for the first time. From the windows of Ednam House can be seen the flat land or haughs watered by Tweed and Teviot where the ram sales are held. As long ago as the reign of King David, that founder of abbeys, a fair was held in the same place, known as St. James's Fair.

The town of Kelso has many personal associations for me. Not only did my grandfather sell his sheep in No. 3 ring at the ram sales, but it was in 'The Cross Keys Hotel' that he made what is probably the shortest after-dinner speech on record, and which I have related in Chapter 1 of this book. One of the last outings I ever had with my father was to the Highland Show when it came to Kelso. For some reason I can remember exactly what I wore on that momentous day. I felt very grand in a brown silk dress patterned with hollyhocks, a white panama hat (with elastic under the chin, of course) white socks and brown shoes with two straps. In the intervening years I have paid many happy visits to the loveliest town on Tweedside. I have backed winners and also-rans at the races, which take place in the spring and autumn, and have even sat in the Mart with a somewhat boisterous companion who gesticulated wildly on the slightest provocation. As we sat on the benches in the Mart I was filled with apprehension in case her arm-wavings were interpreted as bids and that we would be landed with a 'yowe' (ewe) and lambs!

If Kelso is the loveliest town on Tweedside then Dryburgh is the loveliest abbey. It was about five years after the building of Melrose began that the fertile land which borders the river at Dryburgh was marked out as the site for yet another abbey church. Founded for Premonstratensian Canons from Alnwick in Northumberland, this district has strong links with my native county. It was to the Prior of Melrose that the shepherd laddie from Glendale in Northumberland came for instruction in the Gospel. This was the Northumbrian who became his county's most famous man of God, Saint Cuthbert, and who found his resting place where the mighty cathedral of Durham stands today.

Dryburgh lies within a horseshoe bend of Tweed which has wound its way upstream from Kelso. Set in well-wooded land close to the river, this Border abbey has a perfect setting. It is a tragic thought that the work and labour that went into the building of this architectural gem was destroyed like its neighbours by the insufferable Earl of Hertford. Dryburgh survived for almost 400 years until it received its *coup de grâce* from English Henry's henchman in 1545. It is sadder too when one realizes that Englishmen and Scotsmen worked side by side to build it. Monks and masons from Alnwick lived in wooden huts while the walls of the abbey grew higher, and trees from the surrounding woods were felled to make the mighty beams for the rafters. The ruins are of three periods, Norman, Transitional and Early English, which is in keeping with the layout of the abbey which descends by three terraces towards the river.

To Dryburgh in 1832 was brought the body of Sir Walter Scott from his nearby home at Abbotsford. Close to Sir Walter is the tomb of Field-Marshal Earl Haig of Bemersyde, Commander-in-Chief of The British Forces during the First World War. Haigs have been at Bemersyde for 700 years, and the old rhyme says:

> Tyde what may betide,
> There'll aye be a Haig at Bemersyde.

This prophecy still holds good as the present holder of the title and his family live in their ancestral home, the house having been bought by public subscription and presented to the Field Marshal.

The view from Bemersyde Hill was Scott's favourite, and the story has often been told how the horses drawing Sir Walter's hearse paused when they reached the summit, as they had done so often in their master's lifetime. The view from Bemersyde Hill is one of the grandest and most extensive in the Border country. Tweed loops and winds below and in the distance rise the unmistakable triple peaks of the Eildon Hills, landmarks for many miles. Melrose, the abbey of the Cistercians stands above the town of the same name, and far away towards the English Border are the hills of wild Liddesdale.

Dryburgh has probably more visitors than the other great Border abbeys as two of Scotland's most illustrious sons have their last resting place there. This part of Tweedside is often known as Scott country, and streams of visitors flock to the great man's home at Abbotsford. Sir Walter's literary output and his tenacity of purpose fill me with amazement and admiration. Here was an ageing man, never strong and suffering from a physical disability, who worked from six in the morning until six in the evening, in an effort to make enough money to pay off his colossal load of debt. Scott was a traditionalist and a romantic who gloried in the history of his country and his ancestors. It could be said that Scott spoke for the nation and Burns for the people. Scott's sentiments are summed up in his panegyric of patriotism:

> Breathes there the man, with soul so dead,
> Who never to himself hath said,
> This is my own, my native land!

While the ploughman poet retaliates with:

> The rank is but the guinea's stamp;
> The man's the gowd for a' that.

When Scott made his home on Tweedside he was coming back to the land of his ancestors, and where as a boy he had spent so many happy holidays. For six months in 1783 the young Walter went to school in Kelso, the town where in 1803 the Ballantyne Press published the first two volumes of his *Minstrelsy of the Scottish Border*.

Melrose people, should any read this book, will say that I have dismissed their abbey in a somewhat summary manner. For this I apologize, as I am well aware of the importance of this Cistercian foundation. The reason why I have devoted less space to Melrose than to Kelso and Dryburgh is because I do not know Melrose so well, and therefore feel that I am not qualified to write fully on the history of this important Border town. The abbey suffered like its neighbours from the incursions of the English, all the more ironical as the abbey was founded by monks brought from Rievaulx in Yorkshire. In mitigation I can only say that Rievaulx is also a ruin.

This attempt to describe the beauty and historical associations of the Scottish side of the Border is in no way a comprehensive guide, but rather a collection of memories of places I have learnt to love and where I have always been happy.

A Border town for which I have a great affection is Hawick in Teviotdale. Hawick has a completely different atmosphere from that of Kelso; it is a sturdy independent place, famous the world over for its woollen goods and knitwear. My first visit to Hawick, as it was to Kelso, was with my father, and again he was attending sheep sales. I remember hearing a doggerel about Hawick which I may not quote accurately, but it went something like this.

> I like old Hawick and her folks I like,
> Her men and maidens free,
> Sweet memories dwell in the good old town,
> That aye was kind to me.

For some reason this poor little attempt at poetry impressed itself on my childish mind.

I remember that we did not go by way of the Carter Bar on my second visit to Scotland, but crossed the Border at Longtown in Cumberland and reached Hawick by way of the road that runs like a pass through the wild hill country all the way to the strangely named 'Mosspaul Hotel'. Mosspaul is on the boundary line between the counties of Dumfriesshire and Roxburghshire, more than 800 feet above sea-level. About 7 miles from the village of Teviothead the River Teviot has its source, which makes for confusion as one would think the river would rise at its 'head'. Teviot joins Tweed close to the ruins of Roxburgh Castle, and is Tweed's most important tributary.

My first memory of Hawick is a monument which I referred to for many years afterwards as 'The Horse'. The monument is to the Hawick Callants, the rider is the Cornet or Chief Callant bearing a standard aloft. The monument's inscription reads *"Teribus ye Teriodin"*, which was the war cry of the Callants. More than a quarter of a century later I heard the Callants' war cry when I stood in the streets of Hawick in Common Riding Week. (I did not 'let on', as we say in Northumberland, that my home had been in the Hexham district, as the Hexham men were so heavily involved in the sacking of Hawick in 1514, the year after Flodden, an episode I described in *Portrait of Northumberland*.) The Cornet or Chief Callant must be a bachelor and give his word that he will not marry during his year of office. With him is his 'Lass' whom I suppose one could describe as a 'Lady Cornet'. I cannot think of any other name for the 'Lass' who plays such a prominent part in the proceedings. There were ninety-six mounted lads and lasses when I was a spectator in 1959. Hearing the battle-cry "*Teribus ye Teriodin*" shouted repeatedly by the Callants made one realize how intimidating that cry must have been when they rode out to war.

On Friday 5th June 1959 I went to the most extraordinary race meeting I have ever attended, which was Hawick Race Meeting. I have the card beside me as I write and I am not surprised to read that it was held "Under the Rules and Regulations of Hawick Race Committee". It certainly bore no resemblance to any meeting I have ever attended either under Jockey Club or National Hunt Rules. There were nine events on the card, the prizes ranging in value from £80 for the Tradesmen's Handicap to the lowly sum of £2 for the Cornets, which was the eighth on the card, although a silver tankard did go with the £2.

The first race was run at 11.30 a.m. and there were thirty-three entries, top weight was 11 stone 2 pounds and bottom 9 stone 2 pounds, distance "about a mile". In the second race there were thirty-nine entries, rivalling a 'National' field, but as the same horses were entered in so many different events it is almost impossible to count the total number of horses running. The fifth race named the Hornshole Stakes (shades of the Hexham Raid!) was for married and single supporters all carrying the same weight of 11 stone 7 pounds; the entry fee was 2s. The Hornshole, the Pilmuir Stakes and the race for the Cornet's Challenge Cup were the only three on the card in which the jockeys did not wear 'colours', and many and varied were the unconventional costumes of the amateur riders.

Seldom have I enjoyed a day's racing more, unorthodox though it was. The bookmakers were there in full force, some from as far afield as Newcastle upon Tyne. Age was no barrier for the horses, 'aged' and 3-year-olds ran in the same race. I am sure my equine hero and heroine, Doctor Syntax and Beeswing, would have thought they were much too grand to have shown their paces at such a mixed gathering, and blown down their aristocratic noses at the humble horseflesh at Hawick Races. In the words of W. H. Ogilvie in his poem "All the Running":

> It is always good to ride in a race,
> And to win it is always stunning,
> But the proudest thing is to set the pace,
> And make the whole of the running.

My memories and experiences in the Border counties have been many and varied. Brought up as I was, not only on the tales and legends of my own beloved Northumberland, but also on those classics of legend, *Wilson's Tales of the Borders* and Scott's *Tales of a Grandfather*, I have never felt a stranger when I have crossed the Border. Bitter enemies though Northumbrians and Scotsmen have been in the past, the Northumbrian and the Border Scot have much in common, much more than the Northumbrian has with the southern English. It is left to the extremists of the Scottish Nationalist Party to fan the old flames—flames which died long ago with the last smouldering pele-tower in the days of the scorched earth policy.

Since the days when practically every dwelling on the Border was fortified gracious houses have been built as homes, and Mellerstain House in Berwickshire is the most gracious of all. Mellerstain is a creation of a father and son, William and Robert Adam, and is a masterpiece of its kind. One of Scotland's great houses, it is open to the public from May to September and is the home of the Earl of Haddington's heir, Lord Binning. From the terrace of this Border mansion there is a glorious view which stretches to the Cheviot Hills, and—what delighted the writer even more—Northumberland is visible.

An unrepentant Northumbrian, who shall be nameless, has said that the best part of London is the platform at King's Cross where the Newcastle train waits to take Northumbrians home. May I at the risk of offending my Scottish neighbours say that the best thing about the Scottish Border counties is their proximity to Northumberland. To soften this provocative remark I shall end this chapter, as I began, with a verse from Burn's Scottish national anthem, "Auld Lang Syne", in the hope that when I next cross the Border I shall be welcomed with:

> For auld lang syne, my dear,
> For auld lang syne,
> We'll tak a cup o' kindness yet
> For auld lang syne.

15

The Ramblings of the Writer

Forty years on, growing older and older,
Shorter of wind, and in memory long,
Feeble of foot and rheumatic of shoulder,
How will it help you that once you were strong.

Harrow School Song, Bowen

It is with mixed feelings that I write this last chapter of *A Northumbrian Remembers*, and so complete the trilogy I have struggled with for the last five years. My feelings are of relief that at last I have achieved my ambition, and nostalgia for the places and people who have been part of my life for so long. Writing my three books has been a salutary experience; it has made me aware of the appalling gaps in my education, and, to paraphrase Churchill, of "how little I know of so much". The verse from Sir Winston's old school song which I have quoted at the beginning of this chapter seemed to me to be so appropriate for one like myself who started to write when she was 'getting on'. My greatest regret is that my parents did not live to share in whatever success I have had. The inspiration of their memory has spurred me on when I have often felt like giving up.

I have come across an essay written when I was about 12, and a more smug collection of platitudes I have never read. I must have been insufferable, and I am truly thankful that my life has not followed the lines laid down by the 'holier than thou' pious little prig I must have been! I can only think I wrote it with an eye to the future and to impress those who were compelled to read it.

The memories this book, and especially this chapter, have evoked are not in any chronological order, a ramble describes them; but it is a ramble in two senses of the word. In the years I have spent exploring Northumberland I have travelled many miles and my memories cover many years. I have no intention of telling my life story, which is a practice indulged in by far too many people who have written books. What I have tried to do is to link up my personal experiences with my love for my county and its history, which in my case were laid in my early childhood. I am inclined to agree with the Jesuits who say: "Give me the child until it is seven years of age and it is mine for all time." Certainly in my own experience this is true, I have never wavered in my devotion to my family, to the history of my county and my country and to my love of everything connected with rural life. Although the greater part of my adult life, until the last few years, has been spent in a city, I have always remained a country-woman.

The house where I was born, Lipwood Well, is a farmhouse standing beside the Newcastle–Carlisle road (the A69), a mile and a half west of Haydon Bridge. The road has now been widened and the cart-sheds and the railway cottages have been pulled down; the railway runs parallel with the road, though now the diesel trains wail their way along the track, and not the steam-engines of my childhood. The Irish mail train still runs; and in the old days, the 'Paddy' used to rumble on its way with such clatterings that the jug and basin which stood on my bedroom washstand used to rattle in time with the wheels. That same jug and basin is in my house today, and when I first came to Wylam, before the North Line was closed, the vibrations made by the trains had the same effect. Sometimes in that half-world between sleeping and walking I imagined when I heard the rattling that I was a child again at Lipwood Well.

It is practically impossible to write of oneself objectively, and it is so easy to be gifted with hindsight; even diaries are un-reliable and often dull. From early childhood I was a keen diarist, but I doubt if the entries would excite any interest as they are largely composed of such mundane entries as "got up" and "went to bed". I was destined not to be a Pepys or an Evelyn.

I cannot say that my childhood was typical of the period, and certainly it was not the kind of life one would expect a child who was born and grew up on a farm to have led. I was jealously guarded from the facts of life, and for many years I believed that I had been found in a bed of Michaelmas daisies beside the beech hedge! This beech hedge sheltered the kitchen garden from the road, and in the spring it was a nursery for birds' nests.

My good intentions to safeguard the nestlings when they arrived must often have had the opposite effect, and my frequent visits driven the mother bird away. Along with many of the landmarks of my childhood the beech hedge has gone. I used to find the first snowdrops there, while the first primroses were picked in the Round Plantation. The syringa tree my mother planted in what we called the chicken-yard still flowers, and I remember picking blooms to decorate myself as I stumbled about draped in an old lace curtain when I had my wedding craze. This bridal fever was, I imagine, the result of Princess Mary's wedding, as I was (and still am) an ardent royalist. Children have no sense of class-distinction—at least I hadn't, as my bridegrooms, all mythical, ranged from a belted earl to a pitman. After these various marriages numerous offspring were given mass baptisms in the orchard. Many of these incongruous 'children' bore names famous in Northumbrian history. A china doll with blue eyes which opened and shut was Dorothy Forster—this would be after my first visits to Bamburgh and Blanchland. The most dearly loved of all my 'children' was a teddy-bear, now old and battered, who has been my constant companion and now occupies a chair in my sitting-room. This bear was given the proud name of Widdrington, and in my world of make-believe had fought at Otterburn. For some reason my Widdrington's Christian name was Edward. Veracity and accuracy didn't bother me in those days.

One of the great advantages which children of my generation enjoyed and accepted as a matter of course was our safety and security. In some ways the present-day child has more freedom, but we had freedom to wander at will without fear of molestation. My companion on these expeditions, usually to Ridley Woods, was the eldest of a family of nine from the farm of East Mill Hills. This childhood companion is still a friend and on many occasions in the last few years she has driven me to outlying parts of Northumberland when I have been holding forth at meetings. Ridley Woods were a paradise for children, and we used to set off in the morning with our 'bait', bottles of lemonade and, my favourite tipple then, a noxious brew glorying in the name of dandelion stout. The bottles were the old-fashioned kind with 'marble' stoppers such as are never seen now. We used to buy our liquor from the Blacksmith's shop which stood on the road between Lipwood Well and Ridley bridge end. With the passing of the 'heavy' horses these smiths have disappeared, and only a few survive to shoe hunters and 'light' horses. In those days Ridley Hall estate was owned by the Honourable Francis Bowes-Lyon, who was something of an eccentric, and I was always afraid that we would encounter the 'Lion'. I am sure I thought he resembled the stone figures of these beasts that still adorn the gateposts of the drive to Ridley Hall.

The Lees Wood was another favourite haunt of ours, and many were the thrills we had in crossing the swing bridge which then spanned the South Tyne. To reach the river at the bridge we had to walk through one of my father's fields, the 'West Haugh', a field where mushrooms grew abundantly. My mother used to organize picnics to the swing bridge, and if the party was a large one the food used to be taken in a 'long' cart. I used to love making a fireplace of stones, and gathering the kindling sticks, which were usually wet, and the result was that the tea was often smoked. There were no primus stoves and thermos flasks on a Ridley picnic; everything was done the hard way.

I have two vivid memories of these summers beside the South Tyne. One is of my father's sister, Auntie Annie, who would never sit on the ground. What her reason was I never found out. Perched uncomfortably on a shooting-stick Auntie Annie manfully drank her smoked tea, wearing an expression worthy of a Christian martyr. My other aunt, Auntie Peggy, always wore large and unsuitable hats which invariably blew away. No 'lady' in those days ever went out without a hat.

My other memory is one I have treasured all my life, and is of my father sitting with me on his knee by the riverside and telling me the most entrancing stories of animal life. My favourite was one about a family of rabbits who had some amazing adventures, but who always came home safely to their riverside home and were tucked into bed by the mother rabbit, who wore a blue apron. My father was a born story-teller and should have been a writer; his command of the English language was superb. How he would have revelled in Churchill's speeches.

It was from my father that I first heard of those giants of the political past, Gladstone and Disraeli, and in later years of my hero, Grey of Fallodon. I must have been extremely tiresome during this political phase, as I insisted on making speeches on every possible occasion, even if I only had animals for an audience.

Many of the numerous cats were re-christened with outstanding politician's names, while some were even enobled and went to the Lords. When I was creating those imaginary lives for my pets, I little dreamt that for myself some of my flights of imagination would become reality, and that in 1970 I should be a guest in the House of Lords at the centenary dinner of the Josephine Butler Society.

Although I lived so much in an imaginary world, I was also very much of a realist—a trait inherited from my mother—and I revelled in the different seasons of the farming year. I think I loved the hay-time most of all, when we all took our 'teas' to the hay-field. The tea was made in huge cans, rather like miniature milk churns; it had the most delicious flavour (not like the smoked brew of our picnics), and the men drank it out of pint pots. All the food was homemade, scones and tea-cakes, spread with the butter my mother made. We used to sit behind a pike, a sight rarely to be seen now, and when the hay was led home on the bogeys I was allowed to stand at the front beside whichever of the men was in charge of the horse. What infinite patience those men must have had with me, though at times Watson would call me that "little varmint thing". Ned Dodd used to cover up my tracks, if he thought the 'Master' was not in a very good mood.

I loved the thresher days too. I have described in detail what an old-fashioned thresher day was like in an article which appeared in an agricultural supplement some years ago. We always had our meals in the breakfast room on thresher days, a room which was divided from the kitchen part of the house by a green baize door. I was strictly forbidden to open that door whilst the men were having their 'dinners' in the kitchen, but this ban only made me determined to see what went on beyond the green baize door. I did manage to get through, and, nasty little tell-tale that I was, I came back with the news that one of the men was giving pieces of fat meat to the dog. Turning an informer did me no good as I was asked how I knew what was going on in the kitchen!

Sweep the sheep dog who figures in this story slept in a loose-box next door to Pincher, the cob my father used to ride. Sweep had the sweetest disposition of any dog I have ever known. I used to dress him up as one of my historical characters, and the poor thing never once turned on me. I had a very different experience with Moss, who had not such an equable temperament and who snapped at me and caught my cheek with his teeth. I still have the scar.

In those days my father was keenly interested in hens—creatures I have never liked, and I am terrified of clockers, as broody hens are called in Northumberland. I did enjoy watching the chickens tap their way out of the shells in the incubator, and I used to sit, with Blueboy, the Persian cat, beside me, gazing spellbound through the protecting glass as the tiny creatures emerged from the eggs. One of these chickens, a Rhode Island Red, broke its leg, and my mother set it with a match-stick. John, as we called him, decided that as he was not as other chickens are, he could take any liberty he liked, and I remember an uproar when he was caught flying off the tea table with a piece of tea-cake in his beak. After that the green baize door was firmly shut against John and his maraudings. That door which figured so much in my early life suffered badly from the attentions of Blueboy, who decided it was an ideal scratching-post.

As I had a governess until I was 14, I spent my most formative years at home, and I realize now that my roots were planted too deeply. My whole life revolved round my parents, my home and my animals, so that when the break came it was harder for me than for many people. I must say now, in case the wrong impression is given, that neither of my parents were overbearing or possessive, least of all my mother, who was the most unselfish of women. In the years when she was a widow and we lived together in Newcastle, she always insisted that I led a life of my own, and that we should never become known as 'Mrs. Ridley and her daughter'. There was to be no repetition of a sacrifice such as that by Annie Rowell, of which I have already written. In many ways my mother was much more progressive than I am, she lived very much in the present; while I, like my father, am inclined to dwell too much in the past. Yet, to use contradictory terms, it is through my interest in the past that I have been able to make a life for myself. To quote Field-Marshal Viscount Montgomery: "We learn from the mistakes of the past, how to deal with the future." That, in Monty's estimation, is the value of history.

I feel that already I have written too much about my early life, and I have no intention of embarking on a sentimental saga of a country childhood. That subject, like autobiographies, has been greatly over-written. My purpose in writing what I have about myself is to prove that "the child is father to the man" and that our early environment has such a deciding factor on us as people.

At the advanced age of 14 I was sent to a somewhat peculiar (long since defunct) private school in Hexham. Academically the standards were not high, it was still run on the lines of a 'school for young ladies'. Yet had I not been one of its less illustrious pupils, I would never have met one who had a great deal of influence for good on my life. This was the visiting elocution teacher, whose name was Dorothy. She was the most beautiful woman I have ever seen. It was through Dorothy that my interest in drama and poetry was awakened, and in later years, due to her coaching, I was able to pass examinations and earn my living as an elocution teacher myself. On that dreadful day when I said goodbye to my home at Lipwood Well, it was Dorothy who took me and the precious Blueboy to Newcastle. She is dead now, but she is often in my thoughts, and for all she did for me I am eternally grateful. It was at this Hexham 'Academy' that I met so many girls who are now some of my oldest and best friends. What I missed educationally was compensated for by friendship.

How desperately unhappy I was for the first few years in Newcastle, and how I railed against fate. I look back with shame and remorse on my outbursts; then, with the adaptability of youth, I accepted my new way of life, but I realize now that I never became part of it. My heart and interests were always in Northumberland. Newcastle was where I lived, it was never my home in the sense that Lipwood Well had been. During those years I was a voracious reader, and I devoured every book on Northumberland I could find. So determined was I that my mother and I should explore unknown parts of the county, that I managed to save up enough money to buy a second-hand Austin Seven and became an ardent motorist! Distance was no object when BVK 972 took to the road, and we went far beyond the boundaries of our county. What misplaced faith parents have in their children, and what misplaced confidence I must have had in myself. We chugged our way to London by way of Bristol (all rather reminiscent of Chesterton's lines "The night we went to Birmingham by way of Beachy Head") and did the 274 miles from Hyde Park Corner to Newcastle in the record time of nine hours, with stops, of course, for refreshment.

When the war broke out I volunteered as an ambulance driver, and put death on the roads, until I switched over to the less dangerous form of service in postal censorship. For four-and-a-half years I censored the mail, and I am not divulging official secrets when I say that what I don't know about the love-life of the British in wartime would go, in this case appropriately, on a postage stamp. Kipling had something when he said: "The Colonel's lady, and Judy O'Grady are sisters under their skins."

Even during the war years, when transport was so difficult, I managed to get into the country as much as possible. Anyone I met who was a newcomer to the county I dragooned into taking me to my old haunts. Beltingham was always top of the list, a hamlet that is surely one of the most charming in all Northumberland. It was in the church of St. Cuthbert that I was given my baptismal names of Annie Marguerite. For years I have tried to keep this a close secret, and very few people associate Annie Marguerite with Nancy; but, to use a cliché, confession is good for the soul, so I am admitting to the awful truth. When my godfather, Uncle George Pearson, lived at Beltingham I often used to walk there from Lipwood Well, and go to church with him. Beltingham was at one time a domestic chapel of the Ridleys, it is reputed that Nicholas the martyr was christened there.

On 16th October 1555, this most famous of his family died at the stake at Oxford, and made his name immortal. By a strange coincidence I was in Oxford on 16th October 1969, and I took some flowers to the memorial that not only commemorates Nicholas Ridley, but also his fellow martyrs, Hugh Latimer and Thomas Cranmer. The night before the anniversary I was dining with some friends in Oxford who asked me if I intended going to pay homage the next day. When I climbed up the steps of the memorial in the morning I was confronted by a press photographer and a reporter—my friends had 'leaked' the story. I am glad that I made the gesture, as otherwise the anniversary of Nicholas Ridley's death would have passed unnoticed and forgotten, as there is no longer a memorial service held in the church of St. Mary Magdalene.

The day before I paid homage to the martyrs I had been to

Blenheim and Bladon, not only to revive my memories of Duchess Sarah and her great duke, and to see Sir Winston's grave in Bladon churchyard, but in the hope that I could discover something about Sarah Churchill's favourite maid, Grace Ridley. I felt sure that Grace must have had some connection with Northumberland, but unfortunately little is known about the background of this woman in whose arms the 'Terrible Duchess' died, and to whom Sarah left a legacy of £16,000 and her picture by Kneller (now in Earl Spencer's collection at Althorp). All I could establish was that Grace Ridley's father had been a clergyman "somewhere in Oxfordshire". As the Ridley roots are all Northumbrian, I feel sure that Grace's father had 'emigrated'. As I left Blenheim, so intimately associated with the first Duchess of Marlborough, who, until she fell from favour with her childhood friend, Queen Anne, was Mistress of the Robes, Keeper of the Privy Purse and Groom of the Stole, my memories spanned the years and I remembered the day in June 1953 when Queen Elizabeth II was crowned and a very different Duchess from Sarah, Helen, Duchess of Northumberland, was Mistress of the Robes to the Queen Mother. (Duchess Helen held the same position in 1937, when King George VI and his consort were crowned.)

In common with thousands of other loyal subjects I braved the dreadful weather to see Elizabeth II drive through her capital city. Because of the kindness of a friend, I had a seat on the Ministry of Shipping stand in Hyde Park, where I arrived at six o'clock on a cold wet morning to meet a friend from Scotland. As I made my way among the crowds, I heard someone call my name; it was another friend with her husband from Newcastle, and I remember with gratitude that they gave me a swig of rum from a flask they had most wisely brought. As we sat soaked and shivering, but fired with patriotism, I was delighted to recount (in a loud voice so that others would hear) that Northumberland and the neighbouring county of Durham were well and truly represented in the royal entourage. Not only was Duchess Helen in attendance on the Queen Mother but her son, the tenth Duke, carried the Sword of Mercy. One of the canopy bearers when the ceremony of anointing took place was the late Lord Allendale, while the Lord Chamberlain was Lord Scarbrough, who was father of the present Viscountess Ridley, and during the whole of the ceremony the Bishop of Durham shared the honour with the

Bishop of Bath and Wells of attending Her Majesty. I hope any 'foreigner' who heard me was suitably impressed.

Garrulous though this chapter is, I am not going to bore the reader with interminable recollections of things I have done and seen; that kind of thing can so easily descend to the level of name-dropping which seems to be an occupational disease with so many writers. On the other hand it can be most frustrating when one is bursting with some exciting news and held back by the thought that repeating it might be interpreted as swank. It is very difficult to steer a middle course, and a lesson I learnt many years ago when I first appeared before the public is that one must be prepared for criticism. It is impossible to please everyone, and this fact must be accepted. The great asset is a sense of humour and to be able to laugh at one's self. When that goes, then is the time to give up.

Some few years ago I was booked to give a talk to the London Literary Society at the City Temple, which is rather like receiving the public speaker's accolade. I was determined to look my best for such an auspicious occasion, and I asked a friend to make an appointment for me with her hairdresser. I was rather 'gliffed' when she told me that her 'little man' was in Grosvenor Square. Rather above my station in life, I thought. This friend, who is much more worldly and sophisticated than I am, gave me a long lecture on how to behave. According to her I was to 'sweep' into the hairdressers, as though Grosvenor Square was my home ground, and on no account to drop any heather or hay seeds. I therefore did my sweeping act without falling over, and after a very long time, during which glamorous young women and odd looking young men had done their worst with me, I was ready to sweep out, thinking to myself that I hadn't appeared too provincial, when the owner of the establishment, bowing low before me said, "Is Madam going back to the country now?" My exit was a crawl not a sweep!

I only intend to make a brief reference to my speaking life which dates from 1956. Again I was a late starter. I was literally thrown into this hitherto unknown world by an old boy friend, who said, quite truly, that I was mad about history, that I had two diplomas in public speaking and why didn't I do something about it, instead of grinding along teaching elocution, at which I was never very good. I held out against these arguments for a considerable time until I was faced with a *fait accompli* and told that I was to give a talk to a society the next week. The name of the society and the place where they met will remain a secret for all time. It is one of the few places where I have never been asked to go again, and I am not surprised. I was so petrified with nerves that when I did get the first few words out I daren't stop in case I forgot what I was going to say next. How it was I didn't blow up for lack of breath is a miracle. My subject was 'The Rebellion of the '15', though I doubt if the audience realized that I was trying to tell them the story of Derwentwater's bonnie martyred earl. By the time I collapsed into a chair I didn't know what I had been talking about myself. After that dreadful first night, I vowed that never again would I appear before the public. Much against my will I was persuaded to try again, with the result that what began as a challenge has become part of my life.

Dearly though I loved my county, I realized that it was no use confining myself to its boundaries as a speaker, that I must break fresh ground with subjects that would have a general, not only a regional appeal, and so my talks were born: "The Four Queens", "Heroines of History", "Bonnie Prince Charlie" and "Charles II: portrait of a Man". The heroes and heroines of my childhood were to be the bread and butter of my later life.

One day I hope to find time to count up the number of places where I have spoken. It will make a formidable list, as my journeys have taken me to Jersey, the Isle of Man, Scotland and Wales; and wherever I have gone I have met someone from Northumberland. Speaking and writing have given me a full and rewarding life and brought me many friends. When I sat down to write the first page of *Portrait of Northumberland* I had not the remotest idea how to begin, and I remember sitting staring at a blank sheet of paper, until at last the first few words were written. Had I realized the research and the hard work which writing of this kind entails I would have given up there and then. It was my ignorance and obstinacy and my 'I won't be beaten' attitude that kept me going.

I am loath to bring this chapter to an end. I feel I have re-created so much of my life that I had almost forgotten and talked again with the people I have loved so dearly. The grandfather clock which came from Peel Well and is by John Bell of Hexham is ticking away the time. Unless I tear myself away from my gallant old typewriter, which like me has seen better days, I shall be like a speaker I once heard who didn't know when to stop. She raised our hopes many times by looking at her watch, but still soldiered on until at last an old 'body' who could bear it no longer whispered to me, "She doesn't want a watch, she wants a calendar."

At the risk of needing a calendar, I am unable to end, not only this chapter, but this book, without some reference to one of the most exciting occasions I have attended in the last few years. It was in 1964, when I was a guest at a luncheon "within", to quote the invitation, 'The Collingwood Arms' at Cornhill, when the then Prime Minister, Sir Alec Douglas-Home, was the guest of honour. I could scarcely believe that I was shaking hands with Her Majesty's First Minister of the Crown, whose ancestors had fought at Flodden! History had indeed come alive for me at 'The Collingwood Arms'.

When I was a child someone predicted that "All this history with which she fills her head, will be no good to her". Again a prophet has been proved wrong. It is my solace and my *raison d'être*; without it I should be lost.

In my childish scribblings I was very careful to tie up all the loose ends and to impress upon my readers (there were very few) that my literary efforts had come to an end, and I always printed in capital letters that this was so. As I write these last few words of *A Northumbrian Remembers* I repeat what I often wrote as a child: "This is THE END."

Index